Subduing Sovereignty

Subduing Sovereignty

Sovereignty and the Right to Intervene

Edited by
Marianne Heiberg

PINTER
PUBLISHERS
LONDON

Pinter Publishers
25 Floral Street, Covent Garden, London, WC2E 9DS, United Kingdom

First published in 1994

Distributed exclusively in the USA and Canada by St Martin's Press, Inc., Room 400, 175 Fifth Avenue, New York, NY 10010, USA

Marianne Heiberg is hereby identified as the author of this work as provided under Section 77 of the Copyright, Designs and Patents Act 1988.

British Library Cataloguing in Publication Data
A CIP catalogue record for this book is available from The British Library

ISBN 1–85567–267 7

Library of Congress Cataloguing-in-Publication Data
A CIP catalogue record for this book is available from The British Library

Typeset in Discript, London WC2N 4BL
Printed and bound in Great Britain by
Biddles Ltd, Guildford and King's Lynn

TABLE OF CONTENTS

Acknowledgements

In 1990 the Norwegian Institute of International Affairs (NIIA) received a generous grant from the Ford Foundation, New York to carry out a project entitled, "Ethnic Conflict, Peacekeeping and Peacemaking toward 2000: Second Generation Peacekeeping". The aim of the project was to examine the potential future challenges UN peacekeeping could face and to propose some new organizational, military and conceptual doctrines relevant to these challenges. The challenges envisaged in the project proposal included possible enforcement actions under Chapter 7 of the UN Charter, deployment in civil wars in, among other places, Eastern Europe and possible large scale humanitarian interventions.

In the course of two years, the future had become the present and even part of the past.

In May 1992 the Norwegian Institute of International Affairs assembled a small group of eminent scholars and policy makers in Taroudant, Morocco to discuss an issue that is central to the changes currently reshaping international society and the potential role of UN military operations within that society. That issue is sovereignty and the right to intervene.

The workshop was an exceedingly successful and lively one. In addition to the energetic and candid contributions of the participants themselves, the success of the workshop was also due in large part to the special efforts of a wide range of individuals.

NIIA should like, especially, to acknowledge the kind assistance of Mr. Abd-al-Ilah Bennis of the Moroccan Embassy in London, Dr. Assia Bensalah Alaoui, Rabat, and Mr. George Joffe, London. Gratitude is also owed the Norwegian Ministry of Defence and the Norwegian Ministry of Foreign Affairs for their support and the untiring organizational efforts of Mr. Åge Eknes and Mr. Espen Gullikstad, both of the Norwegian Institute of International Affairs. Finally, we should like to acknowledge our long standing debt to the Ford Foundation for its continued support of NIIA's research on UN peacekeeping.

This book is dedicated to the memory of

JOHAN JØRGEN HOLST

Foreign Minister of Norway

who presided over the secret negotiations

between Israel and the PLO

which led to the Oslo Accord

of September 13, 1993.

Johan Jørgen Holst

Uri Savir

Director-General, Ministry of Foreign Affairs

Johan Jørgen Holst has earned a place in the hearts of all who cherish and yearn for peace. His compassion and empathy, as much as his statesmanship, nurtured the atmosphere in which Israel and the Palestinian people could work toward conciliation and peace.

Foreign Minister Holst valiantly undertook a difficult and complex assignment. In facilitating secret negotiations between Israel and the PLO, he helped to overcome decades of tragedy, hostility and mistrust. The abyss between us seemed impassable; Foreign Minister Holst patiently and painstakingly built a stable bridge that we could cross.

We will always remember him for his heartfelt compassion. He opened his heart, allowing us to heal our emotional and spiritual wounds in his home. When the issues we were discussing seemed hopeless, he brought us away from the negotiating table to the warmth of the hearth, allowing us to join in the soothing balm of family life. In the embrace of Johan Holst and Marianne Heiberg, and in the company of their children, we remembered our own families and how we yearned for a true peace so that our children would grow up free from fear. With renewed energy, we were able to continue the difficult work. In time, surrounded by genuine warmth and

1

friendship, there emerged a plan that would, after years of bloodshed and strife, bring the possibility of a real and vibrant peace to Israel and to the Palestinian people.

His patient, quiet and diligent determination, unflagging efforts, and his strategic perspective and view of conflict resolution were the elements we needed to accomplish our work. His abiding love of peace allowed him to facilitate the environment that led to the historic Declaration of Principles between Israel and the Palestinian people, paving the way for conciliation and peace.

Shortly before Minister Holst's death, my Palestinian negotiating counterpart, Mr Abu Alla, and I visited him in the hospital. His voice was broken, but his spirit was whole, and with his unyielding determination he asked us for our ongoing commitment to ensure the implementation of the historic document he helped to bring about and which was distinguished with his own initials as witness. We shall not fail him.

Johan Jørgen Holst has earned an honourable place in history, and everlasting gratitude in our hearts.

In memory of Johan Jørgen Holst

Mahmud Abbas

(Abu Mazen)

member of the PLO's Executive Committee

While I was actually writing the comment below, as an historical testimony of Norway's glorious role in the peace process, I learned of the death of our friend Johan Jørgen Holst. I was shaken, I stopped writing, losing the thread of my ideas and the words and thoughts I had been going to write about him – tears started in my eyes, because I knew that whatever I could say would not match what he deserved. In the end I decided the best way to commemorate him and his country was to continue my account as a testimonial to him.

Norway's Glorious Role[1]

It is a constant source of amazement to me that some tiny thing can cause miracles where something vast cannot. There is no obvious place for Norway among the influential powers of this world for she has had no significant influence either in the old or in the new world order. Despite this, Norway has done something that a giant could never do, and has achieved an

---

1. Also published in Arabic in *Al Wasat*.

3

objective that was beyond the capacities of the superpowers. When we describe what happened in Oslo as an historic event with an outstanding effect on the twentieth century, we must also acknowledge that this small country has played the major positive and effective role in bringing the Oslo Declaration of Principles to the South Lawn of the White House.

It was not our choice nor, I think, of the Israelis either, that Oslo should become a secret channel for negotiations between ourselves and them. But it was a Norwegian initiative which paved the way, first to Israel, which accepted it in principle, and then to a meeting in London where the first contact between the two parties took place. The Norwegians then played a subtle and vital role in bringing the two adversaries together on Norwegian soil. The idea of the secret channel was not new in principle, either for us or for the Israelis. It had been suggested in various ways and by different countries, such as Egypt and Russia, but could not be properly realized on those occasions. The Norwegians, however, were prepared to work at it and to make it work.

It was a difficult mission for all three parties, requiring Palestinians and Israelis alike to observe absolute secrecy in what they said and did. But the Norwegians had the far greater responsibility of controlling events on their own soil and making sure that foreign embassies, news media and intelligence services were not aware what was happening. The mission seemed to be impossible, but nonetheless, it worked. The Norwegians adopted a policy of constantly moving meeting places so that no two consecutive meetings were held in the same place, even in the same city. They also limited the number of people involved in the operation, by putting the whole process under raps and preventing information leaking out, even to people who worked in the Norwegian foreign ministry.

It is not enough for a particular country simply to adopt a policy for that policy to be successful. This certainly applies to the countries of the Third World, but it is equally true for the countries of the First and Second World too. Human nature plays a decisive role in the successful selection and application of policy. Fortunately, the team which supervised the negotiations in Norway had a high degree of enthusiasm and a deep desire for success. Although the motives for actions of this kind are often the personal search for political gain and international reputation, this does not suffice to explain the efforts made by this team. The talks changed the lives of those Scandinavians involved, who usually work in a style and routine that differs completely from our own. But they rapidly adapted to our style and traditions and our conditions. Thus, they worked by night, sometimes until dawn, to ensure that the negotiating process continued. We cannot attribute this simply to self-interest, but to a profound self-motivation and a real concern to make the Middle East peace process work. Many times the Norwegian negotiators were frustrated and disappointed when the talks became deadlocked, but they did not for one moment despair of their ultimate success. The two essential conditions for the success of any undertaking of this kind were present in Norway: reasons of state for adopting such a cause, and individuals who are prepared to devote themselves to this cause willingly and enthusiastically. Norway went beyond the role simply of a host preparing favourable conditions and total secrecy for the negotiators. Its representatives went on to take direct contact with the negotiators to help to bring their positions closer together, offering suggestions, alternatives and new scenarios and acting as full partners to the talks themselves. Their role was not limited by their country's borders; when they needed to move between Tel Aviv, Tunis and Washington – to preserve momentum and continuity and to get first-hand experience of the ideas of the negotiators' leaderships – they did so, trying to convince those leaders that positions could always change at the negotiating table.

Because Foreign Minister Johan Jørgen Holst headed the team for this mission, it seemed that the entire foreign ministry was devoting its energies to this task. The foreign minister did not only depend on his senior officials but took a personal role in following the progress of the talks, watching events, contacting the interested parties and travelling to meet them – while nobody outside the charmed circle even suspected his real mission! The media and international intelligence services were left in the dark about his travels and he cleverly invented pretexts to explain them away.

Now that the agreements have been signed, I note that many Palestinian leaders and cadres have still not read them properly nor digested the ideas and motives behind them. Discussions at leadership and cadre level have revealed that many people do not know the basic assumptions behind the agreements and discuss matters without being in full possession of the facts. We find, on the other hand, that the Norwegian team does know the most minute details of the Oslo agreement and its appendices by heart as well as appreciating its underlying justifications clearly and unambiguously. To us this means that Norway is still completely committed to this operation, not as a neutral mediator but as full partner and arbiter with complete command of the slightest detail of its mission. Norwegian officials were able to prepare the appropriate climate for the original talks, not only narrowing gaps between points of view but also creating favourable personal relationships between the two parties for starting on the new stage – one of coexistence and understanding. This is the stage which started in Oslo and which will be reflected in the future in the Occupied Territories.

Negotiations of this kind are not simply a political dialogue but a mixture of different but convergent interests, sentiments and emotions. At the end there will be either understanding or rejection and, if we abstract the human factor from this process, it becomes soulless and meaningless, even if we do come to an agreement. The agreements that we reached need their proponents to openly support them. That was also the task of the Norwegian team, and was carried out by them with such marked success. There was no difference between the Norwegian foreign minister and his officials in their genuine enthusiasm and desire for results; the officials shared with him the responsibility for following up the negotiating operation. Ter Larsen and his wife Mona, the director of the Minister's Office, were ideal examples of the commitment of foreign ministry officials; they considered the success of this mission to be a personal obligation. I remember that during the talks when the process stalled and looked as if it would break down he collapsed in tears. I do not think he wept because his personal mission looked as if it would fail but because the peace process he supported so fully appeared to be dying. That was another, human, factor in the operation which helped it to be successful and we thank those Norwegians for all they did to make the negotiations a success. The atmosphere of the talks accompanied them even into their homes and families. They lived the talks and the negotiations as an intense personal experience. Without knowing very much of what was going on, they felt they were making history. It showed in their eyes and in the way they welcomed their guests so warmly. They were hosts to the two adversaries in a family atmosphere, free from protocol and its complexities. These human gestures touched the hearts and souls of the negotiators and boosted their enthusiasm.

Mr Holst went twice to hospital for serious health problems. But his suffering did not prevent colleagues from continuing with the peace process, even after the accord was signed, for then they were working towards implementation. Their moral and political responsibilities were not limited by the Washington signing ceremony but has carried on as they insisted that the two parties remove all obstacles in the path of implementation. While Palestinians and Israelis were happy to sign the agreement and while President Clinton and his administration supervised the process, Mr Holst was the godfather to the accord, appreciated by one and all. Many would have liked to be in his place and carry out his mission. One of my colleagues once suggested to me that the Palestinian National Charter defined Palestinians as being born from two Ottoman fathers. He then asked me if Palestinian nationality would be restricted to native Palestinians only. I told him that after such long suffering endured by Arabs and non-Arabs and such sacrifice of time and money, I did not think Palestinian nationality could be restricted to those who were solely of Palestinian origin. Palestinianism has become a political commitment more than a question of origin. So the states and individuals who have done so much to help the Palestinian revolution and made such sacrifices for it have the right to enjoy some recompense in return as an expression of our gratitude. I cannot mention all the hosts of people who have helped us by name; I leave to those who have responsibility in the future for our future the task of giving them their due.

Introduction

Marianne Heiberg

The United Nations is an organization based on the sovereign equality of its members and dedicated to two venerated visions: "to save succeeding generations from the scourge of war" and, "to reaffirm faith in fundamental human rights". Needless to say, the great expectations behind these initial visions have not been realized. Since the signing of the UN Charter in 1945, the world has seen some 50 to 100 inter-state wars. But perhaps the worst carnage and human affliction have not been caused by wars between states, but by wars and tyranny within them. During the Cold War period the UN was relatively powerless to deal with either. For the most part the automatic veto inside the Security Council preempted effective action on the former and the sovereignty of the UN's members implied that the latter was not a polite issue for undue international attention. Despite Charter provisions concerning human rights and the protection of minorities as well as the binding nature of the Charter upon UN members states, with very few exceptions the relation between a state and its citizens has been regarded the *domaine réservé* of the state alone. The changes prompted by the melt down of a global power in Europe has greatly enhanced the UN's capacity to mediate in and act upon inter-state conflict. However, within the UN the possessive insistence on state sovereignty remains to a large degree incompatible with the fulfilment of the second vision to which the Organization is dedicated.

For better or worse the United Nations reflects the realities of the international system in which we live, a system of independent states in which power is very unevenly distributed and rarely exercised with ethical consistency. A system in which appeals to principle may move the heart, but only appeals to national interests are sufficient to move the feet at the expense of state budgets. A system in which respect for state sovereignty remains the cornerstone of international stability. However, the international system and its structuring institutions are undergoing radical transformation although directions of change remain uncertain. One manifestation of this transformation is perhaps paradoxical, but nonetheless critical. A more integrated international system is being forced to confront a distressing, often violent increase in international anarchy. Increasingly, the UN is being requested to act on issues that lie either beyond the frontiers of states, for instance, the environment, or within them, for instance, human catastrophes induced by civil turmoil. Frequently, the most assertive petitioners for action are not governments directly, but the pressure of well organized and articulate Western public opinion groups. The UN's ability to act on these requests is obviously restrained by its resources and the political will as well as interests of Security Council members, among many other factors. Another intrinsic constraint lies in the doctrine of sovereignty and the unacceptability, except under certain extreme conditions, of collective intervention without consent.

Because of the Cold War the collective security arrangements specified in the UN Charter were still born. Instead the UN adopted a somewhat ad hoc, shoe string alternative: UN peacekeeping. Although modest in scope, the achievements of UN peacekeeping should not be underestimated. Peacekeepers were deployed in many of the basket cases of international conflict, for instance, in Cyprus, Kashmir, southern Lebanon and on the Israeli-Arab interface generally. These conflicts sat astride delicate, highly volatile fault lines in regional and often international strategic balances and, thereby, were linked into the towering nuclear risks that underpinned the Cold War.

Not unexpectedly, the conventional wisdoms that sustained peacekeeping mirrored the tight constraints under which the instrument was deployed. Peacekeeping required the consent of the parties involved, usually assumed to be two states rather than shifting alliances of numerous over-armed, local militia groups. It demanded the maintenance of strict neutrality and a clear separation of peacekeeping from peacemaking. In order to distance regional conflicts from the heat of the zero-sum conflict of the Cold War, great powers were disbarred from active participation. What peacekeeping was designed to achieve was highly valuable, but very limited. Above all *limited* peacekeeping was devised to reassure the sovereign states *plenty* involved in conflict, to provide them with, among other things, a face-saving mechanism for disengagement. It was not meant to breach sovereignty either by forcibly containing states or by hoisting an external will or solution upon them.

Currently the trend is to deploy UN military forces in an expanding range of circumstances in which traditional inter-positional peacekeeping is just one. There is a real prospect that the UN will be required to cover a broad scale of activities ranging from nation-building, prevention and deterrence to enforcement and punishment. Increasingly, peacekeepers are also being charged with intervention into what was previously regarded the internal affairs of sovereign countries. They are asked to take over government, such as in Cambodia, monitor elections, such as in Namibia and Angola, and open and maintain humanitarian corridors, such as in Somalia. While in the past few years the challenges faced by the UN have changed dramatically, the conventional wisdoms guiding most UN military operations has not. The distressing performance of the UN in Somalia, the former Yugoslavia, the Western Sahara and Angola, to name some prominent examples, suggest an *reform* urgent need to reexamine the conceptual wisdoms behind UN military operations. And a core wisdom concerns the overwhelming primacy accorded the sovereignty of states.

The end of the Cold War could well mark the logical end to an historic era whose beginnings can be traced back at least to the 17th century. It is an era in which the emergence, multiplication and consolidation of statehood first in Europe, subsequently globally, has been the compelling momentum. This momentum of state building and consolidation has determined the essential organization of international relations and fashioned the core institutions, rules of behaviour and norms that regulate international society. Fundamental to the edifice of current international order is the doctrine of sovereignty, a doctrine which endows state governments with absolute jurisdiction over a specified piece of real estate and exclusive authority over the individuals who reside upon it. It also grants formal equality to all states despite the real and vast disparities in their economic and military power. A corollary of sovereignty is the norm of non-intervention.

Both in theory and certainly in practice sovereignty has always been frayed at the edges, constrained in practice. In theory absolute sovereignty has been limited by, among other things, the laws of war which assert that a state can not wage war in any manner it pleases for mere entertainment. These laws have been viewed as "above" the state and have been accepted by states in theory, if not always in practice.[1] Today even the right to wage war, except in self-defence, is denied states. Generally sovereignty has dealt more with appearances than reality. The doctrine of sovereignty and non-intervention are Western constructs, constructs now most tenaciously affirmed by non-Western states. There are good reasons for this. In practice sovereign immunity from interference is not a question of sovereignty, but of power, a property with which most developing countries are not well supplied.

The rules and norms of international behaviour generated by the doctrine of sovereignty have served the international community well. They have conferred to individual states a sense of dignity, purpose and reassurance regardless of their relative military prowess or population size. Especially for small and weak states, and most states are both, respect for territorial sovereignty and the inviolability of borders remains critical for security and is an irreplaceable attribute for real participation as well as bargaining power within the international community. During the Cold War the principle of non-intervention and the dialogue of nuclear deterrence produced a gridiron within which those states enclosed in the blast centre as well as client states further removed gained unexpected stability.

The order and discipline imposed by the nuclear logic of the Cold War has withered. The landscape ahead is obscure and uncharted. Many former states have disintegrated and fragmented. Many of the fragments have fissoned into fratricide. In addition, the Kantian core is increasingly feeling threatened by pressures, populations and ideologies emanating from regions other than its own. International institutions, and the practices they established, have been overwhelmed by events and are now striving to redefine both priorities and functions.

With the removal of the structuring conflict of the Cold War, the attainment of international security has become more complicated, variegated and elusive. Among other aspects, the rapid proliferation of new states, a process probably far from complete, means that the state centred international system is simply not what it used to be a few years ago. The old, comforting predictabilities of the past have been replaced by a mounting awareness of an extensive range of new insecurities and uncertainties. Broadly, it seems to me that the main sources of current threat lie in four realms all of which are global in scope and all of which undermine the primacy of territorial sovereignty as the carrying pillar of world order. The threats are global in implication and can only be managed by collective remedies. International insecurity will only increase unless a new basis for international society can be found that is appropriate to the circumstances that prevail.

First, the ecological system is severely strained by over-exploitation and an inappropriate use of resources, a trend that can only be exacerbated by current population growth combined with Western consumption patterns. With regard to ozone depletion, desertification and the green house effect, sovereignty is irrelevant.

Second, the interdependent workings of the political economy have already deprived states of large portions of their financial and fiscal autonomy.[2] Even a core state function such as protection of the national currency now lies largely beyond state control. Additionally, the world economy seems to be aggravating inequalities, and hence tensions, both between states and within them. In certain areas, such as Africa and parts of the Middle East, the decline seems irreversible at least for the foreseeable future. Some of the negative side effects include the surging of frustration and despair and the build up of massive migratory pressures.

The third threat involves perhaps the most problematic feature of sovereignty; its absolute linkage to territorial control. Deep structural features within the process of political and economic modernization are among the drives leading to a resurgence of militant, exclusive ideologies some of which have their roots in religious visions, others in inspirations of a secular kind. Albeit with diffrent justifications and aims depending on the case, ethnic militants, of whom religious militants are a sub-category, challenge the current arrangement of state borders and have the power, real or potential, to fracture and transform them.

Because of the ethnic intermingling produced by history, nationalism's insistence on the marriage between cultural groups, linguistically or religiously defined, and territory is increasingly a source of instability and violence between and within states. In order to avoid chaos in the current, uncompleted process of state creation, sovereignty must be untied from territory. We must be able to understand sovereignty in terms other than all or nothing. This is imperative not only for large parts of Europe, but for the Middle East, Africa and elsewhere. Because ethnic warriors, like the ethnic groups they challenge, cannot conceive of political and cultural sovereignty without exclusive control over the territory upon which they live, the logical conclusion is an insistence on either domination or explusion of competing ethnic groups.[3] The notion of territorial sovereignty becomes a formula for ethnic purification, or at least hostile intolerance, when contentious ethnic groups with competing claims to exclusive sovereignty co-exist on the same territory.

The final threat relates to another core issue addressed in this volume. The threat involves the possibility of the prosperous, aggressive Western world oscillating between an ill-considered interventionism and a fortress like isolationism.

To explain: Parallel to international practice and norms

which evolve around the sovereign immunity of the territorial state, another trajectory of international norms, whose origins are also of imposing historical depth, has emerged which evolves around the sovereign immunity of the individual human being. While the concept of sovereignty is fundamental to the conduct of international relations, universal values and standards, such as at least some minimal respect for human rights, also seems to be an increasingly more important condition for world order in an age of mass communications. In an age of transnational standards, the incompatibility between sovereign immunity shielding governments that commit domestic atrocities and influential public opinion concerned with human rights is becoming unsustainable. Perhaps one should recall that France in 1945 proposed an amendment to the UN Charter whereby states which massively violated fundamental human rights would be sanctioned by the withdrawal of recognition of their sovereignty. The proposal did not, of course, gain acceptance. The stability of the international system has required that when respect for state sovereignty proved incompatible with respect for human rights, as has often been the case, the former usually took precedence.

However, particularly throughout the Western world – the part of the world that has the capacity for long range intervention – public outrage, propelled by the mass media, can compel governments to intervene in the internal affairs of other countries. While the pressure on the international community to intervene in, for instance, Cambodia, the former Yugoslavia and Somalia has been close to irresistible, currently no mechanisms that are both effective for the task of large scale intervention and widely regarded as legitimate exist. Thus intervention can occur in manners that are ill-conceived, erratic, ineffective, if not devastatingly counter-productive. Such actions can aggravate the crisis it is meant to relieve, provoke outcries of indignation both at home and abroad as well as discredit the entire notion of multinational intervention. Condemnation could easily nurture an isolationist backlash within Western societies highly detrimental to developing countries as well as to developed ones. Isolation would corrode the tolerance and openness so essential for the well

15

being of Western societies and culture.

As the articles in this volume lucidly show, the issues involved in redefining sovereignty with reference to a right to multilateral intervention are intricate and consensus is lacking. Among other themes, the articles explore the tension between the inviolability of state borders and the inviolability of the individual, the tension between territorial sovereignty and the right to self-determination of minorities, the tension between the North and South with regards to the ethic and legitimacy of intervention and the tension between how the world is and how we might prefer it to be.

Øyvind Østerud, a political scientist, focuses on the evolution of state sovereignty, particularly in reference to competing claims for sovereignty from national minorities. He argues that regardless of the evolution of international law regarding human rights or the right to self-determination, the supreme norm of the international order in the post-Cold War period will continue to be state sovereignty. The orthodoxy of sovereignty remains irreplaceably useful in a pragmatic world shaped by states acting in pursuit of their own national interests.

Jarat Chopra traces the evolution of sovereignty from the viewpoint of international law and reaches conclusions very different to those supported by Østerud. He argues that nonintervention has meaning only in reference to the concept of territorial sovereignty. However, territorial definitions of sovereignty arose in a period which has now been superseded. He suggests that as the exclusive status of sovereignty and statehood are eroded, intervention as a legal concept becomes obsolete. However, Chopra warns that if territorial walls crumble before international law has been strengthened and made enforceable, power and violence could be exercised unfettered.

The article by George Joffe, an historian, reflects the deep anxieties of many developing countries at what they view as an increasingly interventionist world which operates to their disfavour. He charts in particular the growing disillusionment of many third world counties with international organizations which since the end of the Cold War, they believe, have increasing become subservient to the major Western powers and have imposed policies directly detrimental to the third world interests.

Åke Eknes reviews the history of UN intervention and suggests that the UN's right to intervene in domestic affairs is legally far broader than has usually been acknowledged. Moreover, albeit on a limited scale, UN intervention has been relatively frequent. However, he argues that the UN's ability to intervene is highly restricted due to lack of resources and that the system as a whole is open is misuse.

Ernest Gellner, a social anthropologist, examines the mechanics of intervention and non-intervention by analysing tribal dispute mediation in Morocco. He describes a system of mediation, intervention and punishment, common in decentralized tribal society, based on a practice of trial by collective oath (a ritual similar to citing the UN Charter during meetings of the Security Council). In this system guilt or innocence, intervention or non-intervention are determined by keenly considering the balances between interests and principle as well calculating the strengths, cohesiveness, internal tensions and convictions of contending clan groups. Trial by collective oath becomes a means by which the outcome of such deliberations can publicly be justified. The system described closely parallels and gives insights into the modern international order as it has crystallized since World War II.

In the final article Johan Holst summarizes many of the themes that appear throughout the volume and proposes new approaches to the concept of sovereignty and new instruments by which the international community can take some modest new steps in promoting integration and building new communities which transcend traditional divisions.

Notes

1. Peter Calvocoressi, "A problem and its dimensions", in Nigel Rodley, *To Loose the Bands of Wickedness* London: Brassey's (UK),1992 p.2.
2. Stanley Hoffman, "Delusions of world order", The New York Review of Books, Vol. XXXIX, no.7, April 9, 1992.
3. Richard Crampton, "Sovereignty and territorial control are not the same", World Link, Autumn 1992.

Chapter 1

Sovereign Statehood and National Self-Determination

A World Order Dilemma

Øyvind Østerud

The slogan of a "new world order", proclaimed by President Bush during the Gulf crisis, meant first of all the vision of a world in which collective security finally worked: aggressors against international law would be pacified by joint action through the UN. The slogan acquired wider connotations in the immediate aftermath of the Gulf war. US and allied intervention to save the Kurds within Iraq was hailed as heralding a new notion of conditional state sovereignty, limited by universal standards of human rights and moral conduct.

In this context three different principles were already in conflict. First, the principle of sovereign statehood and territorial integrity pleaded by Iraq in defence of exclusive control within its own territory after the Kuwait debacle. Second, the principle of collective action in defence of international law, as legitimized by the series of Security Council Resolutions in late 1990. Third, the principle of human rights across borders, as applied to the Shiite population and the Kurdish minority within Iraq. The idea of non-intervention clashed directly with the demands for international protection of the Kurds.

of the Kurds.

The fate of the Kurds was a strong reminder of the principle of national self-determination as it emerged with imperial dissolution after the First World War. The Kurds narrowly missed sovereign statehood between the treaties of Sevres and Lausanne in the early 1920s. After a period of dormancy, national self-determination generally reemerged as a threat to the established state order with the disintegration of the Soviet Union and the civil war in Yugoslavia. These events are the paramount manifestations of the end of the Cold War. They thus frame the basic context to the whole idea of a "new order"[1]. We shall focus on the complex, triangular relationship between sovereign statehood, self-determination, and human rights; more specifically: is there an emerging "world order" where non-intervention is rendered secondary to international affirmation of self-determination and human rights?

The Ambiguity of Sovereignty

The principle of sovereign statehood hinges on the meaning of "sovereignty" and the criteria of statehood.

The uses of "sovereignty" are murky and ambiguous. They derive from the supreme authority of the *sovereign*, even if no sovereign ever had absolute power internally, and even if sovereign power externally was limited by the sovereign power of others. State sovereignty concerns the international aspects of statehood, and the notion has a substantive and a formal meaning. However, substantive sovereignty is hardly more than a regulative idea. It signifies a material capacity for control of intra-state affairs which always will be a matter of more or less. No state, however powerful, has been self-contained or able to shield its affairs completely from external influence. Sovereignty is often seen as a substantive condition which enables the authorities of each state to be their own master. But in this sense the requirements of full sovereignty have never been met[2].

On the other hand, sovereignty is a formal condition which demands freedom from outside interference. Sovereign statehood here signifies the exclusive jurisdiction of each state. It is a constitutional matter, shielding formal decision making from external authorities. Sovereignty in this sense is a question of all or nothing. As a legal-formal condition it applies to hegemonic superpowers and highly dependent micro-states alike[3].

It is sovereignty in the formal sense which implies the principle of non-intervention. In the modern system of states this is a basic requirement of international law, written into the Charter of the UN. Even sovereignty in this sense, however, is not without legal infringements. The sovereignty of each state is limited by the territorial sovereignty of every other state. The principle of *equal sovereignty* indicates the conditions of sovereign statehood within the framework of international law. Since sovereignty is conditional, there is a potential antagonism between sovereignty and law. One possible exception to the rule of non-intervention is action to protect nationals abroad, although there seems to be an unsettled legal and political debate here[4].

There is wide recognition of state responsibility for the safety of aliens, and particularly for immunity of diplomats, but the scope for forced intervention if rules are infringed is regularly contested. The same combination of formal limits on sovereignty with uncertain sanctions is also evident in other areas. International conventions of minority rights, the rights of indigenous populations, and human rights generally, all deny the unlimited exclusiveness of domestic jurisdiction and sovereign policies, even if extremely few – if any – forced interventions have been conducted behind the banner of these rights. The Kurdish mission in Iraq in 1991 – Operation Provide Comfort – is an exception although the character of the allied operation remains ambiguous.

In terms of human rights in a broad sense there is undoubtedly a contradiction between sovereignty and law. Still the idea of collective military intervention behind legal conventions has not so far eroded the priority of the principle of sovereign statehood. The legal character of statehood itself is a key to this privileged status.

The legally prominent definition of a "state" was given in the first article of the 1933 Montevideo Convention on the Rights and Duties of States: "The State as a person of international law should possess the following qualifications: a) a permanent population; b) a defined territory; c) government; and d) capacity to enter into relations with other states." This definition still has diplomatic standing and is often invoked in deliberations on admittance of new applicants to the club of sovereign states[5]. When the Palestinian Council, for instance, declared the existence of a sovereign Palestinian state in late 1988, the claim was rejected by a majority of Western governments with reference to the Montevideo criteria: the West Bank and the Gaza strip were contested territories without effective Palestinian rule.

The Montevideo criteria indicate that sovereign statehood is granted by recognition based on effectiveness and actual independence. It implies that a state first emerges to fulfil the criteria, and that this empirical entity then is sanctioned by diplomatic recognition. This sequence is, however, a rather one-sided and therefore misleading account of the way states are born.

The Montevideo criteria were intended to solve an increasingly acute dilemma. During the 19th century the status of sovereign statehood had been derived from the political fact of recognition. Diplomatic recognition was not based on explicit rules. Outside the centre-stage of the European state system it was a matter of enhancing a territorial authority sufficiently entrenched to justify normal diplomatic interchange with European powers. The fact of territorial control was transformed to international law through recognition. Recognition was in turn derived from practice – the practice of partnership in treaties, of invitations to inter-state conferences, and by participation in diplomatic exchange with the dominant European states. Some parts of this extended state system were only occasionally recognized, and some were only marginal participants, with no universal recognition-in-practice from all the core members. A system of this type had no definite number of units since the criteria of statehood were largely left undefined.

The state system was based on prescription and customary inclusion until the early 20th century. The doctrine of statehood was ambiguous because recognition could either be interpreted as a practical codification of established status, or as an expression of a practical act which created this status[6]. There was thus a need for workable criteria of statehood on which recognition could be based, independent of the act of recognition alone.

This requirement became urgent with the organization of international peace conferences from the turn of the century (who should be invited?), and of course with the establishment of the League of Nations after the First World War (who could become members?). Admission to the global organizations could not be regulated by mere "recognition", since this was begging the question of universal criteria. Furthermore, it was never assumed that membership as such was a marker of statehood, since independent territories could be admitted by political expediency and since the access of sovereign states could be refused on political grounds. Neither admission to the Hague conferences nor membership in the League of Nations were based on sovereign statehood. Some of the signatories of the League had a clearly dependent status and there was – as we shall see below – a confused debate on self-determination during and after the Versailles Peace Conference. The future implication of the idea of mandate territories also remained unsettled. Therefore, more formalized criteria of statehood were needed. The Montevideo Convention of 1933 was supposed to supply the answer. Here the empirical requirements of recognized sovereignty were declared.

The Montevideo criteria were based on a principle of political effectiveness; actual independence should be established before recognized statehood was granted. Sovereign statehood was transformed from constitutive recognition to recognition as a declaration of empirical qualities. Territorial entities with stable and effective government were further protected by international law: their territorial integrity was a superior right within the system of states.

The Montevideo solution proved to be grossly inadequate in world affairs. A great number of sovereign states have emerged without satisfying the initial requirements of governmental effectiveness. International recognition has also been denied to territorial units which clearly satisfied the empirical criteria. The actual workings of sovereign state proliferation had its origins in the explosive inheritance bequeathed by the Versailles settlement and the League of Nations.

The Antinomies of Self-Determination

The *principle of nationality* had, from the mid-19th century, challenged the inviolability of established statehood. Secessionist movements had evoked the principle in their demand for state boundaries according to "national" – i.e. cultural or historical – criteria. Continental jurists had proclaimed the principle in justification of the fusion of German and Italian principalities. In diplomatic terms the principle was first brought to the forefront by the allied powers – particularly by the United States – as a war aim during the First World War. The doctrine of self-determination had liberal as well as Marxist roots. At the Paris Peace Conference the doctrine was selectively employed to dissolve the Ottoman and the Habsburg empires and to revise European borders at the territorial expense of the powers that lost the war.

However, the League of Nations removed the potential explosiveness of the doctrine. Initial attempts to modify the territorial integrity of states by the Wilsonian principle of self-determination failed. The priority of territorial integrity was firmly codified in the League Charter, and the first test case – the Aaland Islands question – gave precedence to historically established state boundaries above the secessionist demands of peripheral minorities. The League favoured substitute solutions to independent statehood by means of formal protection of minorities. This protection was partly expressed in separate peace agreements between contending states, partly by international declarations in support of minority claims, and partly by a right of appeal to the Council of the League.

European colonies overseas were not included in the diplomatic concern for national self-determination expressed at Versailles and elsewhere.. Although Lloyd George, for one, had occasionally argued that colonial self-determination was included, his views on the rights of indigenous peoples were restricted to the *German* colonies. Allied concern on the whole concentrated on the fate of territories occupied by the axis powers. The post-war mandate system grew out of the problem of German colonies. The idea of a gradual and guided transition towards future self-government for the more emancipated territories was a clever answer to the universalistic implications of "self-determination" on the one hand, and the problem of disposal of the German colonies without subtracting from the ordinary claim of war indemnities on the other. The mandate system was a modest, partial, and incipient program of distant decolonization within the control and final judgement of the colonial powers.

The League of Nations explicitly tried to avoid the ambiguities of the Versailles settlement – as expressed in the final version of the Charter itself and as codified by the Montevideo Convention. However, the idea of national self-determination retained its revolutionary appeal. The mandate system opened up a fissure towards political emancipation. Legally the principle of minority rights made sovereign statehood a conditional and limited quality. In formal terms, and occasionally in practice, there was now a tension between sovereignty and law even if non-intervention remained a superior normative defence line.

The ambiguities of the Versailles settlement, which the League of Nations had strived to curb, were written explicitly into the Charter of the United Nations in 1945. The provisions for minority protection were dropped in favour of the statement that "all peoples" had a right of self-determination. The conflict between effective and stable government, territorial integrity, and a doctrine of self-determination in universalistic terms became acute – even if a "people" with a legitimate claim to statehood remained unidentified.

The UN Charter provided two points of departure for the proliferation of sovereign states after the Second World War. One was the universal idea of self-determination for all peoples (Articles 1 and 55). The other was the provisions concerning trusteeships and non-self-governing territories (particularly Article 73), with an obligation to develop self governing institutions in these territories, and preparing them for a gradual transition from colony to mandate and finally to independent statehood.

The first route was unconditional and universalistic; but intrinsically diffuse, devoid of a clear and uncontested interpretation. The second was a fairly specific obligation to create the empirical prerequisites for effective statehood under the paternal guidance of the colonial powers.

These two programs emerged to become politically acute under pressure of international forces in the 1950s. But they emerged in a radically transformed way, taking the unconditionality of the first idea and the geographical reference of the second one.

Self-determination now became restricted to colonial territories overseas, where decolonization should proceed unconditionally, with a right to sovereign statehood confined to the borders of the colonial territories. The UN doctrine of self-determination-as-decolonization was codified in G.A. Resolution 1514 of December 14, 1960. New proliferation of sovereign states was now restricted to territories across salt water, and further by the colonial delineation of these territories.

Thereby, three alternative notions of sovereignty were brushed aside. First, the idea of territorial integrity put forward by colonial powers like Spain and France, implying that even overseas territories could be legally included within the metropolitan area. Second, the so-called "Belgian Thesis" which denied the validity of the salt water criterion and claimed that *all* non self-governing regions and peoples should be liberated on a par with overseas areas. Third, the ethno-nationalist claim that state boundaries should express the collective identity of cultural groups. The UN doctrine made decolonization into a limited, controlled and predictable process. Territorial integrity and non-intervention were retained for old and new states alike: decolonization should proceed in one step, but only across distant blue water.

The UN doctrine of anti-colonial self-determination had other far-reaching implications as well. The Montevideo criteria of statehood were not required before recognition of sovereignty took place, because decolonization had now become a supreme right. Recognition of statehood was denied if the government of an overseas territory was emanating from descendants of European settlers, even if all the four Montevideo criteria were fulfilled, as demonstrated by the fate of Southern Rhodesia under the Smith regime. The notion of "pigmentational sovereignty" implied that minority rule was tolerated only if the minority had indigenous, or at least of non-European, extraction[7]. Eradication of remnants of across blue-water colonialism had priority even if a clear majority of the population of a contested area chose otherwise, as indicated by the anti-colonial delegitimation of the status of Portuguese Goa in the early 1960s, the fate of the South Moluccans and the people of East Timor after Indonesian independence, and the struggle for the Falkland islands during several decades.

The UN doctrine could not answer the question of self-determination in a definite way. Ethno-national groups reemerged to claim political rights, autonomy or independence within and across the colonial boundaries of new states. Sovereignty as non-intervention continued to protect democratic and despotic regimes alike. Racial sovereignty not only swept aside white settler minorities from power, but also formed a shelter for indigenous repression and dictatorships. The international conventions on human rights again indicate the antagonism between sovereignty and law. What are the odds for these concerns within the present state system? We shall first explore the idea of collective rights on a non-state basis.

Sovereign Rights and National Rights

Sovereign statehood is codified by the doctrine of non-intervention. A state may be composed of a rather haphazard collection of people, without collective identity, mutual bonds or group character outside the authority of the state. The principle of nationality is an idea to rectify the arbitrary composition of states by introducing a new basis for political legitimacy. The problem with this alternative basis is the notorious issue of the "self": "the people cannot decide until somebody decides who are the people".[8] "Nationality" outside state citizenship – in ethnic or cultural or historical or subjective terms – is ambiguous, amorphous and variable. It can hardly make a firm legal foundation for sovereignty since there is a wide variety of national markers and a historically contingent flux of demands for statehood.

The "logic of national liberation" has no stable solution in terms of statehood and sovereignty. First, there are areas where any geographical boundary would cut across group identities or ethnic markers because the population is mixed or changing. Decolonization has in itself shown the weight of this problem, where literally no state has been too small to contain a secessionist movement. Second, national minorities often have their own minorities, as shown by the fate of Hindus in Pakistan, Moslems in India, English-speaking Canadians in Quebec, etc. Not only has every African state its Katanga, but even Katanga has one, as Moise Tchombe experienced in the early 1960s. Third, the liberation of one national group is often the repression of another. Group rivalry about the same territory, as in Northern Ireland or the West Bank of Jordan, implies that any liberation is biased. National delineations according to different criteria – history, colonial unity, religion, language, or ethnicity – may contrast in a way which implies that contending parties all wave flags of national liberation, as exemplified in Indonesia or the Western Sahara. Furthermore, ethno-national secessionist movements have great historical plasticity and fluctuating strength as expressed by regionalist mobilization in advanced industrial societies.

It has been estimated that sovereign statehood for ethno-national groups would produce a world of several thousand states.[9] The concept of nationality may be even more ambiguous than suggested by such estimates. A *principle* of national self-determination would be quite revolutionary.

These pragmatic arguments for the territorial integrity of states do not preclude pragmatic arguments for secession or autonomous minorities. The degree of repression or disorder may indicate that split sovereignty is a more legitimate and viable solution. It is possible to argue for national self determination on specific merit even if the *principle* of national self-determination is ambiguous and untenable in its general form.

Still one crucial question remains: should internal repression – of national minorities or other groups and individuals – indicate that non-intervention no longer applies?

Humanitarian Intervention

There has been some international argument about the right to intervene militarily in defence of nationals abroad. Great powers have occasionally argued in support of intervention, like the US in Grenada in 1983. However, the idea of a right has been turned down in several General Assembly Resolutions, basically because it could be employed as justification for intervention for other reasons. Non-intervention has been the supreme UN norm.[10]

However, there are hardly any examples of forcible intervention under the humanitarian flag of protection against repression and human rights violations. When India intervened in Bengal prior to the establishment of Bangladesh, or Vietnam in Cambodia during the Khmer Rouge period, or Tanzania in Uganda during Idi Amin's reign, their arguments were in terms of counter intervention or security threats, even if convincing grounds for humanitarian action could have been put forth. Even more, no country has advocated a principle of unilateral humanitarian intervention as this would open a Pandora's box in inter-state relations.

What about collective intervention authorized by the Security Council? Is this the possibility that unfolded in the last stages of the 1991 Gulf War, stimulated by Iraq's repression of its Kurdish and Shiite population?

Politically collective security – even if mobilized by the United States – formally had worked for the first time since the Cold War no longer immobilized the Security Council. The Council, however, did not circumvent Article 2(7) of the UN Charter by authorizing intervention to protect human rights,- not in Kuwait and certainly not in Iraq. All Security Council resolutions before and during the Gulf War authorized the use of force to remove Iraqi forces from Kuwait and to restore "international peace and security".[11] Also the deployment of US, British and French forces in Northern Iraq in April 1991 was within this authorization, since S.C. Resolution 688 of April 5 found that the consequences of Iraq's repressive policies, including the flow of refugees across the Iraqi-Turkish frontier, threatened peace and security beyond Iraq's own territory.

Military intervention by allied forces in Iraq, subsequently replaced by UN forces, was not legitimized as purely humanitarian intervention. To the extent that humanitarian motives played a part, it may be argued that intervention served to save the political dividend of Operation Desert Storm in face of international public opinion. The major allied powers were initially eager to apply the rule of non-interference strictly, once the Iraqi forces were out of Kuwait[12]. The Gulf War and its aftermath in no way imply that humanitarian intervention is currently an operative principle in international affairs.

Neither do the revolutionary events in Eastern Europe – and the dissolution of the Soviet Union – mean that sovereign statehood is modified by the principle of nationality. The Soviet Union dissolved from within. Recognition of new states like the Baltic republics was not granted until imperial control was virtually abandoned. No foreign power ever considered enforcing Baltic liberation.

The Yugoslav crisis is somewhat more complicated. Here foreign recognition of Croatia (and Slovenia) took place in the midst of civil war, but UN intervention – preceded by muddled EC mediation – aimed at a cease-fire which rested on consent from contending parties. Some European countries, like Germany and Italy in this case, seemed to sympathize with national self determination based on cultural markers. But permanent Security Council members, like the United States, Russia, France and Great Britain, were eager to reiterate that no support of such destabilizing principles obtained. The civil war and its potentially disruptive regional spill-overs were the major reasons for international concern and interference. Not even the Yugoslav crisis indicates that the principle of national self-determination as against sovereign statehood, or the idea of external enforcement of human rights, have gained international priority. Yugoslavia had already dissolved from within in a protracted civil war when international organizations intervened. Political considerations tipped the balance in favour of national break-up, in contrast to the outcome of the Biafra war or other post-colonial secessionist crises.

The dissolution of multi-national communist states has demonstrated the legitimacy crisis of sovereign statehood, but this crisis was well advanced in many post-colonial states also during the Cold War. The principle of the sovereignty and territorial integrity of states does not seem to be fundamentally shaken by recent events.

The international human rights movement has also effected conventions which deny the complete sovereignty of established governments. These conventions are not, however, supported by instruments of enforcement. In this respect there is now a wider gap between sovereignty and law, but there is hardly a new order in which law actually infringes upon the exercise of sovereignty.

Conclusion; or Why the Kurds of Iraq Lost

Sovereignty and non-intervention constitute the supreme norm of the international order also after the Cold War. There is nevertheless a conceptual dilemma between sovereignty and law, with the idea of universal human rights on the side of unenforced legality.[13] The principle of national self-determination, on the other hand, oscillates within this dilemma. It is pleaded by sovereign states when they are threatened by external forces, and it is pleaded as a right of autonomy or secession by internal forces threatened by repressive state authorities. Demands for self-determination from one side are constantly met by corresponding demands from the other. Considerations of order, originating from the fact that international relations are based on a state system, have a bias in favour of sovereignty.

The Kurds of Iraq lost because intervention on their behalf was not an application of a general principle of humanitarian intervention or support of national rights. Intervention occurred, half-heartedly, because international opinion threatened the dividends of the war, because there was a risk of chaos across international borders, and because the initial forced intervention against Iraq took place in a context shaped by great power interests. These factors meant that the limits of support for the Kurds were quite narrow.

The basic general obstacle to humanitarian intervention is perhaps that it never can be isolated from wider repercussions. It is bound to affect the very political fabric of the countries concerned, be they Iraq or Yugoslavia. Here again sovereignty contradicts law, with arguments for self-determination floating between the opposite horns of the dilemma.

Notes

1. Freedman, Lawrence, 1991/92, "Order and Disorder in the New World", *Foreign Affairs*, Vol. 71, No. 1.
   Hoffmann, Stanley, 1992, "Delusions of World Order", *The New York Review of Books*, Vol. XXXIX, No. 7, April 9.
   Mayall, James, 1991, "Non-intervention, self-determination and the "new world order ", *International Affairs*, Vol. 67, No. 3, July.
   Mayall, James, 1992, "Nationalism and International Security after the Cold War", *Survival*, Spring.2.
   Hannum, Hurst, 1990, *Autonomy, Sovereignty, and Self-Determination*, University of Pennsylvania Press, Philadelphia.
3. James, Alan, 1986, *Sovereign Statehood*, Allen & Unwin, London.
4. Asrat, Beltchew. 1991, Prohibition of force under the UN Charter, Uppsala, IUSTUS, 1991.
5. Crawford, James, 1979, *The Creation of States in International Law*, Clarendon Press, Oxford.
6. Crawford, James, 1979, *The Creation of States in International Law*, p 17ff, Clarendon Press, Oxford.
7. Mazrui, Ali A. 1967, *Towards a Pax Africana*, Weidenfeld and Nicolson, London.
   Jackson, Robert H. 1990, *Quasi-states: sovereignty, international relations and the Third World*, Cambridge University Press, Cambridge.
8. Jennings, Ivor, 1956, *The Approach to Self-Government*, Cambridge at the University Press.
9. Gellner, Ernest, 1983, Nations and Nationalism, Basil Blackwell, Oxford.
10. Akehurst, Michael, 1984, "Humanitarian Intervention", in Hedley Bull, ed, *Intervention in World Politics*, Clarendon Press, Oxford.
11. Gardner, Richard N. 1991/92, "International Law and the Use of Force", *Adelphi Papers* 266, IISS, London.
12. Mayall, James, 1992, "Nationalism and International Security after the

Cold War", *Survival*, Spring.

13. Berman, Nathanael, 1988, "Sovereignty in Abeyance: Self-Determination and International Law", *Wisconsin International Law Journal*, Vol. 7, No. 1, Fall.

Chapter 2

The Obsolescence of Intervention under International Law[1]

Jarat Chopra

Suez; Hungary; Czechoslovakia; Afghanistan; Grenada; Panama; Kuwait. These names speak for themselves, even out of context and without qualification. The reader immediately recognizes them as instances of intervention, as expressions of the appetites of power and the willingness to violate both territorial boundaries and the integrity of law. They have entered the collective imagination as symbols; to speak these names is to evoke meaning beyond geography and conjure dramatic images of tanks, troops and violence. Widely condemned in each case, they became symbols of wrongfulness.

The lexicon of international law is similarly filled with words that evoke more than their ordinary meanings: self-defence, aggression, genocide, human rights, self-determination.[2] Curiously, "intervention" does not sit in the company of these terms. While Suez, Czechoslovakia and Panama suggest meaning beyond meaning, almost mythically, "intervention" does not. It is not properly part of the language of international law, despite its frequent usage.

The reason for this is significant. The principle of non-intervention is not spelt out in the United Nations Charter and although it can be discerned in customary international law,[3]

intervention is not a crime in the manner that law refers to the
peremptory crime of aggression or the crime of genocide.
Intervention is unlawful not by itself, but because non-
intervention is a logical corollary to the concept of territorial
sovereignty. Exclusivity over territory and the idea that none
can trespass on the private property or interfere in the
independence of another are implications of sovereignty and
its personification in the form of the state.

Consequently, the parameters of the non-intervention norm
shift as sovereignty and statehood are redefined, or more
properly un-defined. Both sovereignty and statehood as legal
terms are undergoing an identity crisis, a crisis so fundamental
that the special role of states as the principal global actors is
likely to be displaced. While neither term has been rendered
irrelevant, a trend that has been gradual and continuous
throughout this century[4] suggests a declining future for both.

As the exclusive status and inviolable nature of sovereignty
and statehood are eroded, intervention as a legal concept is
rendered obsolete. Intervention implies crossing boundaries,
but as the identity of states as states becomes indeterminate,
frontiers cease to have limits and borders evaporate. This does
not mean that the actions which have been categorized as
intervention cease to occur. They do not. But the perception of
them as "intervention" withers away. If armed force is used, it is
unlawful not because it is an intrusion, but because the use of
force is prohibited; if humanitarian assistance is delivered
during a famine, it is not a transboundary act, but the fulfilment
of an international legal right to life. The challenge of
international law today is to reconceive its prohibitions and
obligations beyond a territorial context. That is, the selective
application of law, regulating acts between territories but not
within territory, is no longer sustainable.

This was dramatically illustrated in the Security Council
debates preceding passage of Resolution 688 in the wake of the
1991 Gulf War. UN member states insisted "that Iraq allow
immediate access by international humanitarian organizations
to all those in need of assistance in all parts of Iraq and to make
available all necessary facilities for their operations."[5]
Supporters of the resolution could not reconcile sovereign

inviolability with the need to defend human welfare. They retreated to the position that 688 was upholding both; they did not try to redefine either and argue that the protection of human rights was not a violation of sovereignty. Instead, they linked human rights with international peace and security.

Unable to reconcile the inviolability of territory with the need to intervene, the Security Council relied on a justification that transcends territorial exclusion, and which does not fit neatly between borders. Though not without controversy, it is apparent that if peace and security, human rights or the degradation of the environment are to be regulated by law that can legitimate action, then they cannot be considered subject to territorial limitations. In January 1992, the first Security Council summit meeting issued the following statement:

"The non-military sources of instability in the economic, social, humanitarian and ecological fields have become threats to peace and security. The United Nations membership as a whole . . . needs to give the highest priority to the solution of these matters . . . They recognize that peace and prosperity are indivisible and that lasting peace and stability require effective international cooperation for the eradication of poverty and the promotion of a better life for all in larger freedom."[6]

It is this trend towards indivisibility of global problems on the one hand and indeterminacy or identity crisis in international law on the other that renders intervention as a concept unworkable.

However, there is an obvious danger in an international society without boundaries. May not unrestricted freedom of movement serve the will of the powerful at the cost of the weak? Does the list of exceptional wrongs cease to be symbolic and instead becomes the order of the day? In the absence of hindrances are not the appetites of power whetted even more?

An indivisible international society is not a prescription. It is an inevitability, and nothing is a more potent imperative for strengthening the security system of the United Nations than this inevitability. UN forces will find it increasingly difficult to assume that the world in which they operated, with clearly identifiable parties in conflict consenting to a Security Council mandate, will be a reality in the future. Exceptions such as the Congo and Cyprus are already becoming the rule. Military fronts compete with juridical frontiers and render indeterminate boundaries in places like Bosnia, Somalia and Cambodia.[7]

In a new world reality what will be the challenges for UN forces and the Charter generally? Both will have to overcome the fiction of a world composed fundamentally of states. The use of force by national liberation movements, insurgents and terrorists shifted the nature of warfare. Since the Second World War, the incidence of inter-state conflict has been significantly less than conflict between governments and armed groups independently organized.[8] Non-governmental organizations, with which the UN is increasingly cooperating,[9] have become significant players in the areas of human rights and the environment.[10]

Post-Cold War rhetoric has spawned a phantom "new world order". Paradoxically, a new world order is emerging but it bears little resemblance to the proclaimed architecture.[11] Cold warriors and analysts who had simply got it wrong proclaimed 1989 *annus mirabilis*. Revolutions in Eastern Europe were not miraculous but a consequence of redefining boundaries of authority in which individuals and peoples could and would inevitably become actors beyond governments, even though they themselves may not have realized the underpinnings of their actions.[12] Others were more aware of underlying trends:

"International society is the society of the whole human race; international law is the law of international society. This has revolutionary implications: it means to take power out of the hands of states and put it in the hands of people. As we conceive international society as society and no longer consider states as sovereign equal persons, then this [transfer of power] solves itself."[13]

The choice is clear: either reconceive international law or face more "miracles."

The Norm of Non-Intervention

Legal debates concerning the non-intervention norm have focused on the permissibility of exceptions to the rule.[14] These include: assistance to the authorities of a state by invitation; assistance to rebels by invitation; humanitarian intervention for the protection of nationals and non-nationals; and more recently, intervention to overthrow illegitimate regimes and intervention to combat terrorism and drug-trafficking.[15] However, these categories are becoming increasingly artificial as the interpretation of the non-intervention norm focuses more on the nature of the act than on its transboundary character.

In 1949 the International Court of Justice (ICJ) rejected the notion that there exists on the part of states a right of intervention. The Corfu Channel case between the United Kingdom and Albania concerned a minesweeping operation by the Royal Navy in Albanian territorial waters against the clearly expressed wishes of the Albanian government. The United Kingdom claimed its right to do so without consent. This was not accepted:

> "The Court can only regard the alleged right of intervention as the manifestation of a policy of force, such as has, in the past, given rise to most serious abuses and such as cannot, whatever be the present defects in international organization, find a place in international law. Intervention . . . would be reserved for the most powerful States, and might easily lead to perverting the administration of international justice itself.[16]

The Court did not elaborate further on the definition of intervention but instead reminded the United Kingdom Agent that "Between independent States, respect for territorial sovereignty is an essential foundation of international relations."

This did not prevent attempts by East and West blocs to influence the outcome of rebellions seeking to overthrow colonialism during the 1950s and 1960s. To combat neo-colonial influences[17] the UN General Assembly passed Resolution 2131 (XX) on 21 December 1965, the "Declaration on the Inadmissibility of Intervention in the Domestic Affairs of States and the Protection of their Independence and Sovereignty."[18] Although still affirming a blanket prohibition on state intervention, this outlined the kinds of acts that were not permitted. Article 1 condemns "armed intervention and all other forms of interference or attempted threats against the personality of the state or against its political, economic and cultural elements." Under Article 2 "no state shall organize, assist, foment, finance, incite or tolerate subversive, terrorist or armed activities directed towards the violent overthrow of the regime of another state, or interfere in civil strife in another state." Enumerating prohibited forms of intervention left open the possibility that other acts not expressly listed may be permissible. It also meant that the prohibition was not just regarding the fact of intervention but pertained to kinds of acts.

In the 1986 Nicaragua case, although the Court referred to the Corfu Channel decision and the 1965 Declaration, in its own deliberations it emphasized the unlawfulness of the kind of intervention at issue and not the fact of intervention: "Intervention is wrongful when it uses methods of coercion ... The element of coercion, which defines, and indeed forms the very essence of prohibited intervention, is particularly obvious in the case of an intervention which uses force."[19]

By referring to "prohibited intervention" the Court implied that there could be cases of non-prohibited intervention, and that the distinguishing feature would be whether the act was prohibited by another provision of international law. In this case, US involvement in military and paramilitary attacks in Nicaraguan territory constituted a breach of its obligations under international law not to use force. The Court noted, however, that an unlawful intervention did not have to involve the use of force. The US supply of funds to the contras was undoubtedly prohibited as an intervention in the internal affairs of Nicaragua, but it did not amount to the use of force. The wrongfulness here was not merely the provision of funds, nor merely the fact of intervention, but the goal of the United States to overthrow the Nicaraguan government – a clear form of coercion.[20]

The elasticity of "intervention" as a concept and the increasing focus on the legality of 'the act' have fanned the debate regarding permissible forms of intervention. This is illustrated by the expanding notion of humanitarian intervention. Although by no means universally condoned, the ICJ in the Nicaragua case confidently asserted that "There can be no doubt that the provision of strictly humanitarian aid to persons or forces in another country, whatever their political affiliations or objectives, cannot be regarded as unlawful intervention, or as in any other way contrary to international law."[21] As such, had US assistance been given indiscriminately, and "not merely to the contras and their dependents," it would have escaped condemnation regardless of the fact of "intervention."

The larger significance of judging 'the act' rather than the fact of intervention is to break down territorial boundaries as a barrier to the universal application of law. However, despite this fundamental shift there is a limit to the evolution of intervention as a perspective since it is a part of something else, of sovereignty and statehood. Although this jurisprudential trend exhibits an internal erosion of sovereignty, it is the external status of sovereignty that determines the outer limits of non-intervention.

A Genealogy of Sovereignty[22]

"If you can comprehend the idea of property or the idea of slavery, you can easily comprehend the idea of sovereignty. Like sovereignty, property and slavery both involve the ideas of exclusion and of authority."[23] To accept sovereignty is to create the notion of intervention and to accept the impermissibility of intervention as a challenge to both exclusion and authority. In this way sovereignty is the source of international boundaries and constructs city walls around countryside. Walled territory becomes the physical form of the state, which as an abstract identity, a self, necessitates the existence of 'the other.' And 'the other' is something to be excluded.[24]

But while the state has an identity, sovereignty does not; while sovereignty erects boundaries, sovereignty itself has no boundaries. The theory of sovereignty is entirely incompatible with territorial limitations and frontiers. This essential flaw in the idea of territorial sovereignty has not prevented the creation and perpetuation of physical boundaries. Far from it: during the period of decolonization boundaries were erected and regarded overnight as inherent, unchallengeable. These fictitious lines were maintained not by a flawed theory of exclusion and authority, but by a collective imagination and a zealous faith in a common state identity. This self-deception of peoples meant a belief that rule from within the state was self-rule: "we are sovereign"; and by "we" was meant ruler and ruled. But as the imagination of peoples are stimulated by increasingly complex living conditions, as identities are reformed, the simple formulations, flawed as they are, of sovereignty and statehood become irrational. In the tribalism of Europe and Africa,[25] and even America,[26] sovereignty and territory part company.

Sovereignty is a particular kind of authority. It is a theory that refers to (1) power that is above the law and (2) the fiction that the ruler and ruled are integrated. Sovereignty is not a fact, like energy or power. It is a characteristic and it is not measurable as more or less. It is definitive and does not permit derogation without being rendered illogical. As an absolute beyond reproach, sovereignty provides finality and determinacy in the international system. In other words, it creates order. Order means predictability and while the immutability of sovereignty meant reliability, through its incapacity to change, the formula of sovereignty is becoming unworkable.[27] This is apparent if the present moment is placed in a historical context.

The origins of sovereignty lie in the Roman Empire. The Hellenistic monarchies were restricted by the Greek notion of law as something more valid than the community or its rulers. As such, the king "personified law" since his will amounted to the rules of order. This was a departure from the divinity of the ruler in the Near East and ancient India, where the king may have governed by the grace of gods but was, like his subjects, subordinate to the external laws of the universe, or dharma. In the Roman Empire, however, it was argued that if there is a source of law then it must be above the law. Consequently, the Emperor was regarded as "above the law; and by the law was now meant the codes, customs and constitution of the society itself. These are the essential elements in a theory of sovereignty and it was now, from about the end of the first century AD, that they were first enunciated."[28]

Roman sovereignty was not only final and absolute but by definition it meant that "no final and absolute authority exists elsewhere." In this sense sovereignty was a logical consequence of an empire that had physically unified the known world, and for that matter extended into the heavens since the emperor was himself considered a god. If there was a final point of authority, it was reasonable for it to be absolute. And in this universalized world, "intervention" had no meaning.

The Middle Ages were characterized by fragmentation. Despite attempts to unify and centralize authority, such as by the Carolingians and the Holy Roman Empire, large concentrations of secular power never attained the distinct feature of sovereignty. Its metaphorical implications of immutability, inviolability, perfection and transcendence were monopolized by the church, on which the emperor relied for legitimacy. Interestingly, while Roman identity had a universalist tendency, logically, and was based on the oneness of Roman citizenry, identity in Christendom was also universalist and based on the oneness of mankind. Complete territorial unity and complete territorial disunity fostered comparable world views.

The first articulation of the modern theory of sovereignty, and consequently the origins of the possibility of intervention, appeared in 1576 in Jean Bodin's *De la république*. It came in an unprecedented context, during a conflict between the universal empire and local kings claiming supremacy on the basis of Roman law. The king was proclaimed to be Emperor within his own kingdom and "had of right all the attributes – including the power to interpret the law and to make new law – which, on the basis of the same Roman law but in relation to all Christendom, the Roman lawyers were claiming for the Emperor and the canon lawyers were claiming for the Pope." Christendom could not withstand the physical unification occurring locally as communities became increasingly organized and integrated. It was only a matter of time before authority was linked exclusively to territory.

Bodin's sovereignty transformed this linkage into an absolute. It was initially formulated as a reaction to the civil and religious wars in France at the time of the Reformation. A Protestant right of resistance and rebellion based on customary and divine law was pitted against Roman law and Divine Right asserting the absolute powers of the French crown. Bodin sought to restore harmony to the political community by integrating the ruler and ruled in the body politic. This was a search, as others had done before and still others would do afterwards, for the finality and determinacy that had characterized the Roman Empire. Although he rejected the immorality of Machiavelli's *raison d'état*, Bodin gave him his due, for Machiavelli had sought to reconcile the prince and the community and concluded this was only possible by the total absorption of the community by the unfettered will of the ruler.

Bodin "feared anarchy more than he disliked tyranny." Sovereignty was not absolutism that operated in a vacuum, capable of disregarding all laws. It was meant to be limited by "the nature of the body politic as a political society comprising both ruler and ruled." In effect, it was an abstraction that fostered the perception of indivisibility of ruler and ruled. It did so by elevating the link to an absolute and metaphysical plane, comparable to the final point of authority in the Roman Empire. Both were subsumed under a common identity so complete that delinkage could not be imagined. It was a fictional integration that was sustained by popular perception. The linkage of the ruler with delimited territory and the ruler with the ruled created the conditions for state identities which were similarly abstract and elevated and therefore capable of apparent unification.

There were two shortcomings of this neat package. First, the fictitious nature of the integration of the ruler and ruled meant that while some superficial construct had been finalized, the distribution of power within that construct was not. This has fostered revolutions and civil wars ever since. Despite – or perhaps because of – the rise of parliaments, Rousseau's popular sovereignty[29] and the revolutions of the late eighteenth century, sovereignty became the sovereignty of the ruler, of government. (Surely this primacy of the ruler over the ruled would lead to a norm prohibiting intervention to protect human rights.)

The second theoretical difficulty with sovereignty was that it operated as a closed system and could not account for the existence of other sovereigns – for the very reason that it did not have to in the Roman Empire. Kingdoms designed with imperial patterns bred imperial habits. It seems an inevitability that they created empires abroad and fought with one another at home. Absolutes with limited territorial boundaries could only lead to war, as they have done in ever increasing intensity. War has been the natural consequence of an irreconcilable logic backed by the social power of 'imagined communities.'[30]

The world has outgrown this irreconcilable logic, the image of solidarity between ruler and ruled and the exclusivity of territory that this relationship engendered. The principle first enshrined in Article 2(1) of the UN Charter of sovereign equality between states was a necessary reaction not only to the multiplicity of sovereigns, which by their plurality meant none could be properly sovereign, but to the absurdity of proliferating sovereigns of disparate sizes and strengths. The universalist tendency of the Roman absolutes, already confined by territorial boundaries, had less and less breathing space outside these boundaries as this proliferation proceeded. More sovereigns meant more restrictions on each, even on the powerful with regards to the weak and the small – at least nominally. If pressures of conflicting sovereigns were to be withstood in any practical sense, even if there seemed no logic to the contradiction, unmitigated non-intervention had to be accepted by all and the derogation of this considered sacrilege. But it was the nature of these extra-territorial pressures, despite the persistence of designated physical borders, that there would begin an integration, an interdependence. States, small and large, may have been Roman Empires on paper but they could not pretend to have such independence in fact.

Integration and interdependence naturally meant physical interpenetration and a crisis for the inviolability of territorial frontiers.[31] Just as technology had been a unifying force for local kingdom communities in Christendom – the printing press, for instance, had consolidated official state languages, and therefore artificial national identities[32] – it continued to have a unifying influence on a grander scale.[33] The advent of the atomic age, the idea that missiles from Omaha or Omsk could reach their targets not in hours but minutes, extinguished the distance between destruction and the destroyer. Today's satellites that traverse "space above any territory of the globe, regardless of 'sovereign' rights over air spaces and duties of 'non-intervention,' serve to emphasize the new openness and penetrability of everything to everybody."[34] The "open skies" regime permitting military overflights of sovereign territory as a confidence-builder is a recognition of the mistrust and danger that exclusive boundaries can foment.[35] The growth of civil aviation has necessitated the participation of territorial sovereigns in a network of air links which are now difficult to sever.

Just as territorial frontiers can no longer exclude influences, they can no longer contain pressures. The movements of peoples, either by force of circumstance as refugees or by the increasingly accessible luxury of air travel, is occurring on an unprecedented scale. What is the territorial identity of an ethnic diaspora of the likes of the Tamils located in southern India, northern Sri Lanka, Europe and the Americas? This is a delinkage (psychologically and physically) of population from territory. Electronic communications and media have fostered conscious and unconscious identification among all humanity.[36] That the most powerful economies in the world, the G-7, must act in concert on major policies reflects increasing awareness of global financial integration. Interconnectedness has entered the consciousness of public opinion and has been expressed through popular concern for the environment, human rights and health – including the AIDS epidemic.

The internationalization of sovereign "state-territory as a species of property"[37] has begun. "The common heritage of mankind," enshrined in the 1979 Convention on the Moon and Other Celestial Bodies, the 1982 Convention on the Law of the Sea and the 1991 revision of the Antarctic Treaty, "marks the passage from the territorial postulate of sovereignty to that of cooperation."[38] This was a shift from the idea that these open spaces belonged to no one, which therefore permitted the powerful an advantage in their exploitation, to the perception that they belonged to everyone, thus regulating conduct on an equitable basis.

If this shift takes place with regards to protection of the environment, territorial sovereignty will become effectively obsolete. The hypotheses proposed in the late 1970s[39] that the earth behaves like an organism, a single living system, accentuated the superficiality of political boundaries. While popularly received, they were not views shared by governments. But the inability of states to respond in any effective way to the threats to life posed by the degradation of the environment[40] culminated in the global summit of June 1992, the United Nations Conference on Environment and Development (UNCED) where an "Earth Charter" was debated.[41] Governments recognized that cooperation is indispensable, but they were not willing to forego significant disagreement. It may be that cooperation will only be achieved through designating the environment part of the common heritage of mankind.[42] This would so fundamentally restructure the conception of territoriality that intervention would become irrelevant. It would mean turning, inevitably, to a universal away from an inter-national system. Just as abstract Christendom could not withstand the physical unification of local kingdoms, the abstractions of sovereignty and statehood are challenged by this trend towards universal physical unification.

With the evaporation of territorial boundaries, what does sovereignty become? If it ceases to have physical expression, is it any more than an attempt to determine finality in the linkage of ruler and ruled – in other words, only a psychological phenomenon? If an absolute becomes partial; if what is supposed to be above and immune from the law is increasingly eroded by the law; if a unitary structure is forced to operate relatively, then what is the logic behind retaining the services of sovereignty? The personification of sovereignty is the state, and while the erosion of sovereignty erodes the validity of the principle of non-intervention, the identity crisis of the state raises the question of what is being violated by intervention.

Undefining Statehood

Charles Taylor refers to the "malaise of modernity," a kind of post-modern identity crisis within Western society in which relativism and extreme individualism, isolated self-definition, have fostered fragmentation. He is concerned with the resulting "ethical inarticulacy." Populations have self-defeated themselves: fragmented and unable to coalesce around a common purpose and form a common will, people have failed to govern themselves even in – particularly in – the most democratic societies. As members of a fragmented society "find it harder and harder to identify with their political society as a community,"[43] the delinkage of the ruler and the ruled becomes apparent. Consequently, in a powerless community government governs easily, without effective leadership, paternalistically – Taylor refers to Tocqueville's "soft" despotism. The identity of the state, no longer the identity of territory or the population, becomes the identity of government, or more properly of government officials.[44] An international law reserved for states becomes international law for government officials. This is an unsustainable proposition for law in a universalizing world.

This identity crisis of the state is causing the legal concept of statehood to become undefined under international law. This is occurring in two ways: through the delinkage of population, territory and government described above and through a shift in the ingredients of the statehood formula. The consequence of non-statehood has meant the preponderance in the international system of non-state actors and widespread fragmentation, indeterminacy and inarticulacy. A post-modern world without clear boundaries renders "intervention" obsolete.

Article 1 of the 1933 "Montevideo Convention on the Rights and Duties of States" defined statehood as possessing four qualifications: (a) a permanent population; (b) a defined territory; (c) government; and (d) capacity to enter into relations with other states. The first three are the concrete forms of the state while the fourth, an abstraction, is the affirmation that these in combination constitute a state. "Capacity" in this sense is recognized sovereignty. These characteristics of the state are quantitative qualities. If the concrete ingredients existed as facts, then a state was said to exist and could participate as a subject of international law. If any one was missing, then the whole package did not exist according to law. This is more true of the creation of states since the test of statehood is stringent, the burden of proof high. But once a kind of critical mass point is reached then the three concrete qualities are fused and catapulted through recognition to a sovereign status. Once affirmed as a state, the burden of proof of losing this status, because of the untouchable nature of sovereignty, is even higher. If a government collapses, as in the Congo in the 1960s, Lebanon in the 1980s or Somalia in the 1990s, or if territorial boundaries are in flux, as the borders of Israel still are, then statehood persists. Sovereignty maintains the fusion even as the criteria delink.[45]

Over time this formula was challenged and certain qualitative characteristics were added. Not only did the factual criteria have to be present, but their combination had to be of a certain kind: Was there a willingness and ability to observe international law? Was the regime in power racist or unlawfully constituted? Was independence achieved in accordance with the principle of self-determination?[46] Was the prohibition on the use of force violated? This represented a shift from an objective set of criteria for defining statehood to a subjective test of legitimate statehood.[47]

In the meantime, a shift in the opposite direction occurred with regards to the practice of recognition. There are two basic theories of recognition: constitutive and declaratory. According to the first, "it is the act of recognition by other states that creates a new state and endows it with legal personality." In other words, a state exists because other states say it exists. The declaratory theory "maintains that recognition is merely an acceptance by states of an already existing situation. A new state will acquire capacity in international law not by virtue of the consent of others but by virtue of a particular factual situation."[48]

The policy of governments shifted from the more subjective constitutive approach to dependence on objective criteria of statehood in the declaratory theory. The boldest statement to this effect was by the UK government in 1980. In the House of Lords the Foreign Secretary, Lord Carrington, announced that following "a re-examination of British policy . . . [and] a comparison with the practice of our partners and allies . . . we have decided that we shall no longer accord recognition to

Governments. The British Government recognizes States in accordance with common international doctrine."[49] The practice of Great Britain had been to recognize governments on the basis of effective control of territory, but also as a form of approval. Recognition of government and statehood was synonymous.

Carrington's statement was an attempt to distance recognition from a form of approval. There was a need to enter into relations with governments which the UK did not approve of or did not want to appear to approve of. The catalyst for the shift in this case was the human rights abuses in Ghana following Britain's recognition of the government of Lieutenant Jerry Rawlings in 1979. It was also the practice of other governments. The United States had made its statement in 1977.[50]

By recognizing the state as distinct from government the UK was establishing an objective process of recognition. It implied that recognition virtually occurred by itself, on the basis of the facts. But this presupposed that there was an adequate checklist of objective criteria on which to base recognition devoid of judgement. This was not the case since there had been a marked shift from quantitative to qualitative characteristics of statehood. This constituted, in fundamental terms, an identity crisis. If the legitimacy of the state was tested subjectively, but the acceptance of the state as a state relied on objective criteria, how did the state become? How did it cease to be? The state had undefined itself.[51]

This phenomenon is coupled with a physical fragmentation of the state as population, government and territory are delinked. This is particularly apparent as individuals and peoples become independent actors internationally, as international law becomes directly applicable to them, and as state governments are circumvented as a filter for international relations. The reference points of identity shift from the state as a community to the community of the nation, of an indigenous population, an ethnic diaspora, an expatriate community, the family, the region, the North or the South, or to the individual in the community of mankind. In some cases the location of these may match state boundaries; in most cases they will not. The diaspora or the common community of mankind have no territorial boundaries. While these have been gradual trends, the implications for international law are quite revolutionary, since to accept the existence of non-state actors under law means that the state loses its exclusive place. As an abstraction it becomes no more than a corporation without the inviolability that sovereignty implies. Without a sense of inviolability, intervention has no meaning.

Law is a closed system that creates its own reality metaphorically. It creates order by regulating relations between subjects. Subjects are characterized as having rights, such as the right to sue in court to have grievances redressed, and duties, such as the duty to act in accordance with the law of the land. Under national law, individuals and organizations are considered subjects, while possessions – such as a table, a car or an animal – are categorized as objects. Objects have rights and duties only in so far as their owner, as a recognized subject, accords them. When law recognizes an actor as a subject, it is said to have gained personality. Personality, by itself, does not define who or what the actor is or should be, only that it is identified as having the capacity to act under law, to hold rights and perform duties. For instance, when a business becomes incorporated under national law, it secures the legal status of an individual and has the right to sue in court and the obligation to abide by the law. International law has traditionally differed from national law in its definition of subjects and objects.

In this way human beings have been treated as mere possessions of states, traditionally the principal subjects of international law, and according rights and duties to individuals is to jeopardize the exclusivity and authority of the state. The turning point in this process was the Nuremberg Tribunal. In his opening remarks Justice Jackson, Chief Prosecutor for the United States, argued the necessity to accord international criminal responsibility, and therefore personality, to Nazi defendants:

"The wrongs which we seek to condemn and punish have been so calculated, so malignant, and so devastating, that civilization cannot tolerate their being ignored, because it cannot survive their being repeated. That four great nations, flushed with victory and stung with injury stay the hand of vengeance and voluntarily submit their captive enemies to the judgement of the law is one of the most significant tributes that Power has ever paid to Reason . . . The refuge of the defendants can be only their hope that international law will lag so far behind the moral sense of mankind that conduct which is crime in the moral sense must be regarded as innocent in law."[52]

The Tribunal rejected the defense relied upon by the Nazi war criminals that they were immune from prosecution since they had acted as agents of the state, and as they had no standing under international law only the state as a construct could be held responsible. It argued that "international law imposes duties and liabilities upon individuals as well as upon states" because "crimes against international law are committed by men, not by abstract entities, and only by punishing individuals who commit such crimes can the provisions of international law be enforced."[53]

It followed that if individuals had duties under international law then they could claim rights. In 1948 the Universal Declaration of Human Rights and the Genocide Convention affirmed this[54] and since then there has been a continuous struggle to define the width and breadth of "human rights," as well as to devise mechanisms for their enforcement.[55] The battle lines have been clear: humanity and the state. "In so far as the denial of the fundamental rights of man has been associated with the nation-State asserting the claim to ultimate reality and utterly subordinating the individual to a mystic and absolute personality of its own, the recognition of these rights is a brake upon exclusive and aggressive nationalism which is the obstacle, both conscious and involuntary, to the idea of a world community under the rule of law."[56]

Tragically, for forty years human rights have been relegated more to a process of definition than enforcement. They "were quickly appropriated by governments, embodied in treaties, made part of the stuff of primitive international relations, swept up into the maw of an international bureaucracy." But "the idea of human rights having been thought . . . cannot be unthought. It will not be replaced, unless by some idea which contains and surpasses it."[57] The conception of human rights has challenged the territorialization of the earth by transforming the solidarity of mankind from an ideal into a necessity, and by emphasizing a common human identity through definition of a basic human condition. Particularly, it is a condition articulated not only by rights such as "to life, liberty and the security of the person,"[58] but it includes the right to have rights, internationally and universally.

However, it is also true that the human condition is a social condition; human beings organize everywhere they are, and while individuals may be basic building blocks it is not clear what will be the basis of their groupings. What will be the basic unit of an evolving international society? Article 18(1) of the 1981 "African Charter on Human and Peoples' Rights" states that "The family shall be the natural unit and basis of society." Some argue it is the nation, others see culture as an organizing principle; political ideas or ethical values may be the basis of communities. Fundamentalist faiths will have their own kingdoms of gods and political parties. In this way, physical "place" is pitted against conceptual "space."

Something of an answer may emerge from what is referred to as the third generation of human rights, the rights of peoples.[59] Defining "peoples" was a practical problem faced during decolonization by attempts to implement the right of peoples to self-determination referred to in Articles 1(2) and 55 of the UN Charter. What constitutes the "self"? The ICJ interpreted it narrowly and defined "self" strictly as a people under colonial domination.[60] Under international law this restrictive definition has been challenged by references to self-determination in the former Soviet and Yugoslav republics, and curiously in the Cambodian peace agreements of October 1991.[61]

The "self" can be redefined outside the colonial context and widened in its application.[62] However, the limits of this are difficult to discern. For instance, one goal of self-determination has been sovereign statehood. But if a "self" gains personality and overthrows government control, then another person within that self may do the same, and so on. In this way, Croatia may claim independence on the basis of self-determination, but so may its Serbian minority. For this reason international law has never recognized a right of secession.[63]

This popular chasing of sovereign statehood accelerates fragmentation. If self-determination is to result in self-governance, then it can no longer be conceived as a means to statehood. The first casualty of self-determination has been self-definition. The artificial boundaries of Africa are a testament to this. The first goal of self-determination and the only apparent response to this international malaise is to recognize an underlying, on-going search for new bases of social identity. In this regard, Sir Crispin Tickell, former British ambassador to the United Nations, stated that "The old notion of sovereignty as a wall around a nation-state has simply crumbled . . . And that must be a good thing."[64]

United Nations Forces

This is the new reality in which United Nations forces must operate. At the end of the Cold War and as the UN enters its second institutional generation, these conditions pose an apocalyptic image and emphasize the potential for chaos and anarchy, the indiscriminate uses of force and unfettered exercises of power, for "nothing is so conducive to international violence as the fears and appetites that breed on inequality and instability and on the knowledge that these things exist."[65] Unlike Bodin, we must not fear anarchy more than we dislike tyranny, since these conditions may not be so apocalyptic. They are the natural consequence of an international self-development and fear of this is really only attachment to familiar global structures whose time has come. But the threat of violence is real: Human beings live, die and kill for identities.

If the United Nations is to ensure the safe passage of this process with its inherent capacity for self-destruction, then there must be a recognition of these challenges. With the erosion of territorial boundaries, "intervention" may pass from the lexicon of international law but the acts categorized as intervention do not cease to occur; they are likely in fact to multiply in number. The United Nations is not a saviour. It may not be able to provide the kind of security that fragmentation necessitates, but as it reforms it will have to respond to these underlying currents if it is to be effective, if it is to fulfil the kinds of tasks it has already taken on. If it can rise to the occasion, the UN may provide the best means for stability until some organizing principle emerges. It will have to become the mechanism for underwriting a universalizing international law as a transition mechanism. This means preventing or reacting to unlawful acts on the basis of those acts alone, irrespective of geography. Coercion, disturbances of the peace, human rights abuses and perhaps even terrorizing the environment will be cause for UN action; not invitations by the perpetrators of the crime.

Consent to the presence of UN forces will wither away with the concept of intervention. The UN Secretary-General, Boutros Boutros-Ghali, reported that the United Nations Protection Force (UNPROFOR) in Yugoslavia would complete its task regardless of the opinion of the parties in conflict.[66] It was not possible to obtain consent from any authority in Somalia before the UN and United States deployments there.[67] The concept of preventive diplomacy was enunciated in September 1988 in a Soviet aide-mémoire circulated at the UN entitled "Towards comprehensive security through the enhancement of the role of the United Nations." Drafted by then Deputy Foreign Minister V.F. Petrovsky, it proposed that UN observers be stationed along "frontiers within the territory of a country that seeks to protect itself from outside interference at the request of that country alone."[68] In this case consent could not be obtained from the other party without it admitting its posture was threatening. The proliferation of conflicting parties and general fragmentation in Lebanon prevented the United Nations Interim Force in Lebanon (UNIFIL) from relying on consent to its operations as long ago as 1978. In any case, Chapter VII of the UN Charter is a basic affirmation that the aggressor abrogates its right of concession; the nature of the crime supersedes the consideration of non-intervention.

Increasing inability to determine who the parties in conflict are or to obtain consent of any legitimate kind forces UN operations to be constitutionally based on the UN Charter alone. While consent had always been a practical necessity in peacekeeping because of the defensive posture of lightly armed troops, it was never a legal requirement. Bowett argues that whether a state is a host or providing transit facilities for an operation, it is obliged to concede to the requirements of the United Nations. Article 2(5) obliges states to assist the organization when undertaking action in accordance with the Charter; Article 25 obliges states "to accept and carry out the decisions of the Security Council in accordance with the present Charter"; and Article 49 similarly obliges states to "join in affording mutual assistance in carrying out the measures decided upon by the Security Council." Having already conceded to these commitments, no further explicit consent of states to the presence of a peacekeeping operation on their territory or to the character and composition of the force is required. Indeed, as "peacekeeping" does not appear in the Charter, there is no explicit legal requirement for consent.[69]

The ICJ affirmed in the Reparations case that the United Nations could rely on implied powers, not expressly provided in the Charter, as being essential to the performance of its duties.[70] For instance, Article 1(1) states that the first purpose of the United Nations is: "To maintain international peace and security, and to that end: to take effective collective measures for the prevention and removal of threats to the peace, and for the suppression of acts of aggression or other breaches of the peace, and to bring about by peaceful means, and in conformity with the principles of justice and international law, adjustment or settlement of international disputes or situations which might lead to a breach of the peace." According to this, "the UN was intended to have, and has, abundant unexpressed powers in matters relating to world peace."[71]

Halderman argues that all peacekeeping operations are "collective measures." Concern for consent or express "procedural authority for a particular armed forces action has obscured the more fundamental consideration of the substantive creation of power [under Article 1(1)] to perform the central function for which the United Nations was created."[72] The constitutional basis for UN forces, therefore, is found in Articles 1(1), 39 and 42. He distinguishes "collective measures" from "enforcement measures." Both involve the use of armed forces under the central direction of the organization – as representatives of the collective will – in a manner similar to the ideal chain of command in a collective security enforcement action, but may differ in objective, character and composition.

Halderman offers three propositions in his thesis: (a) that there is no Charter authority for UN forces other than that pertaining to collective measures, even with the permission of the countries concerned; (b) that such forces must meet the requirements of collective measures; and (c) that once they are properly so constituted, there is no Charter requirement that permission for the movement of such forces be obtained. Similarly, Bowett and Doswald-Beck add that consent of governments do not render as lawful those acts that are generally considered to be illegal.[73]

Will the United Nations be able to effectively underwrite this Charter-based authority and apply international law as an interim measure of stability? It will have to enhance its military capability, which will require significant assets from the major powers to be placed under UN control.[74] Mandates and instructions to armed forces must become clearer and more specific without emasculating the flexibility of operations. The legitimacy and authority for these instructions must derive from a common interpretation of the Charter and international law. This will have to include assessing restrictions on the use of force by UN forces. Proportionality in enforcement requires quantification. As security problems are redefined, so must the meaning of "collective" be reconceived to include the will of non-states.[75]

Conclusion

The legal concept of "intervention" sits uncomfortably between the disintegrating exclusion of territorial boundaries, these legal lines in the dirt becoming unravelled. State boundaries represent the unity of a government, its population and territory, and their inviolability as a construct. As this imagined linkage is eroded, the identity of the construct and its boundaries become indeterminate, and intervention ceases to have logical relevance. Concurrently, international law is increasingly applied to acts regardless of geography. The general prohibition on the use of force, the growth of a human rights regime and prospects of environmental protection overshadow territorial limits to the application of law.

There is potential for grave danger. If territorial walls crumble before international law has been strengthened and underwritten by United Nations security forces, violence will be widespread as power, no less by the small than by the large, is exercised unfettered. The challenge is to recognize these underlying trends and move in a post-modern age beyond the territorial definitions of an early modern period.

Notes

1. I am grateful to the following individuals for comments on earlier drafts: Robert McCorquodale, Cambridge University; Nicholas Onuf, American University; and Adam Roberts, Oxford University.
2. On the creation of social reality through words, see Philip Allott, Eunomia: New Order for a New World (Oxford: Oxford University Press, 1990), ch. 1.
3. Military and Paramilitary Activities in and against Nicaragua Case, I.C.J. Reports 1986, para. 202. Hereafter referred to as the Nicaragua case.
4. For an earlier call to end sovereignty, see Harold J. Laski, The Grammar of Politics (London: G. Allen & Unwin Ltd., 1925).
5. See further on debate behind SC Resolution 688, "Security Council Demands Iraq End Repression of Kurds, Other Groups; Calls Civilian Plight 'Threat to Peace and Security,'" UNDPI Press Release, SC/5268 of 5 April 1991.
6. "Note by the President of the Security Council," S/23500 of 31 January 1992, pp. 3 and 5.
7. Cf. Sir James Eberle, "International Boundaries: the security angle," The World Today, April 1992, pp. 68–71.
8. See further, Thomas M. Franck, "Who Killed Article 2(4)?" 64 American Journal of International Law 1970, p. 809; and Heather A. Wilson, International Law and the Use of Force by National Liberation Movements (Oxford: Clarendon Press, 1988).
9. See for instance, in the field of humanitarian assistance, Larry Minear et al., Humanitarianism Under Siege: A Critical Review of Operation Lifeline Sudan (Trenton, NJ: Red Sea Press, Inc., 1991). See also the terms of the Special Coordinator for Emergency Relief Operations in

Liberia (UNSCOL) described in UN Doc. A/46/403.

10. See for instance, respectively, David Weissbrodt, "The Contribution of International Nongovernmental Organizations to the Protection of Human Rights" in T. Meron, ed., Human Rights in International Law: Legal and Policy Issues (1984), pp. 403–430; and Philippe J. Sands, "The Environment, Community and International Law," 30 Harvard International Law Journal 1989, p. 393. See also the special role of NGOs at the United Nations Conference on Environment and Development (UNCED), "Partners for Sustainable Development," UN Doc. A/CONF.151/PC/100/Add.13.

11. On defining US President George Bush's version, see Steve Brinkoetter, "The Role for Ethics in Bush's New World Order," Ethics and International Affairs, vol. 6, 1992, p. 70.

12. See also James N. Rosenau, "Normative Challenges in a Turbulent World," Ethics and International Affairs, vol. 6, 1992, p. 2.

13. Philip Allott, lecture in the "Law of Peace," Cambridge University, 26 October 1987.

14. See generally, John Norton Moore, "The Control of Foreign Intervention in Internal Conflict," 9 The Virginia Journal of International Law 1969, pp. 209–342; and Louise Doswald-Beck, "The Legal Validity of Military Intervention By Invitation of the Government," 56 British Year Book of International Law 1985, pp.189–252.

15. On these latter categories, see Lori Fisler Damrosch and David J. Scheffer, eds., Law and Force in the New International Order (Boulder: Westview Press and the American Society of International Law, 1991), ch. 13–16 and 21–24.

16. Corfu Channel Case (Merits), I.C.J. Reports 1949, p. 35.

17. On this interpretation of the origins of the norm of non-intervention, see Doswald-Beck, "Invitation," p. 252.

18. The essentials of this resolution are repeated in Resolution 26 25(XXV) 1970, "Declaration on Principles of International Law Concerning Friendly Relations and Co-operation Among States," which the General Assembly declared to be "basic principles" of international law.

19. Nicaragua, para. 205.

20. Ibid., para. 241.

21. Ibid., para. 242. On the conditions for genuine humanitarian assistance see para. 243.

22. See also, Jarat Chopra and Thomas G. Weiss, "Sovereignty is no Longer Sacrosanct: Codifying Humanitarian Intervention," Ethics and International Affairs, vol. 6, 1992, pp. 95–117.

23. Allott, Eunomia, para. 15.37.

24. For example, on the difficulty of overcoming images of 'the other' as 'the enemy,' see Eduard Shevardnadze, The Future Belongs to Freedom

(London: Sinclair-Stevenson Ltd., 1991), ch. 4, and Working Together (Providence, RI: Thomas J. Watson Jr. Institute for International Studies, 1991).

25. See particularly Basil Davidson, The Black Man's Burden: Africa and the Curse of the Nation-State (New York: Times Books, 1992); as well as Isaiah Berlin, "The Bent Twig: On the Rise of Nationalism" in The Crooked Timber of Humanity: Chapters in the History of Ideas (New York: Vintage Books, 1992), pp. 238–261.
26. See for instance Arthur M. Schlesinger, Jr., The Disuniting of America: Reflections on a Multicultural Society (New York: W.W. Norton & Co., 1992).
27. Consider the statements of former UN Secretary-General Javier Perez de Cuellar in "The Limits of Sovereignty," UNDPI/1178, February 1992.
28. F.H. Hinsley, Sovereignty, 2nd ed. (Cambridge: Cambridge University Press, 1986), p. 41. The quotes below are from pp. 26, 88, 122 and 125.
29. Although note that notions of popular sovereignty had an earlier lineage, first with radical elements in the medieval church and then with radical protestants. Cf. Otto Gierke's *Political Theories of the Middle Age* and *Natural Law and the Theory of Society, 1500–1800*. I am grateful to Nicholas Onuf for pointing this out.
30. See generally, Benedict Anderson, Imagined Communities (London: Verso, 1991).
31. On change as being for the first time on a global scale, see Alexander King and Bertrand Schneider, The First Global Revolution: A Report by the Council of the Club of Rome (New York: Pantheon Books, 1991).
32. See further, Anderson, Imagined, ch. 5 and 6. See also Eric Hobsbawm, Nations and Nationalism since 1788 (Cambridge: Granta Publications Ltd., 1990).
33. See further, Ithiel de Sola Pool, Technologies Without Boundaries: On Telecommunications in a Global Age (Cambridge, MA: Harvard University Press, 1990), ch. 6 and generally.
34. John H. Herz, quoted in R.P. Anand, "Sovereign Equality of States in International Law," Receuil des Cours, 1986-II, pp. 31–32.
35. See for instance, Michael Krepon and Jeffrey P. Tracey, "'Open Skies' and UN peace-keeping," Survival, vol. XXXII, no. 3, May/June 1990, pp. 251–263.
36. Marshall McLuhan, The Gutenberg Galaxy: The Making of Typographic Man (Toronto: University of Toronto Press, 1962), and Understanding Media: The Extensions of Man (London: Routledge & Keegan Paul Ltd., 1964). See also, Cynthia Schneider and Brian Wallis, eds., Global Television (New York and Cambridge, MA: Wedge Press and MIT Press, 1991).

37. Allott, Eunomia, para. 16.65.
38. Antonio Cassese, International Law in a Divided World (Oxford: Clarendon Press, 1986), p. 391. On the concept of "the common heritage of mankind" generally, see ch. 14.
39. James Lovelock, Gaia: A New Look at Life on Earth (London: Oxford University Press, 1979); James Grier Miller, Living Systems (New York: McGraw-Hill, 1978).
40. See further, World Commission on Environment and Development, Our Common Future (New York: Oxford University Press, 1987), p. 22.
41. Preparatory Committee for the United Nations Conference on Environment and Development, "Principles on General Rights and Obligations," A/CONF.151/PC/WG.III/L.8/Rev.1, 30 August 1991.
42. Cf. "common concern of mankind" and "vital interests of mankind" referred to in the Declaration of the Hague, 11 March 1989, cited in Sands, "Environment, Community," pp. 117–120.
43. Charles Taylor, The Malaise of Modernity (Concord, Ont.: Canadian Broadcasting Corporation/Anansi, 1991), p. 117. See also Sources of the Self: The Making of the Modern Identity (Cambridge, Mass.: Harvard University Press, 1989). Compare these with John Kenneth Galbraith, The Culture of Contentment (New York: Houghton Mifflin Co., 1992).
44. Philip Allott, "State Responsibility and the Unmaking of International Law," 29 Harvard International Law Journal 1988, p. 16.
45. See generally, James Crawford, "The Criteria for Statehood in International Law," 48 British Year Book of International Law 1976–77, pp. 93–182.
46. On democracy as a basis for legitimacy, see Thomas M. Franck, The Power of Legitimacy Among Nations (Oxford: Oxford University Press, 1990), and "The Emerging Right to Democratic Governance," 86 American Journal of International Law 1992, pp. 46–91.
47. See further, James Crawford, The Creation of States in International Law (Oxford: Clarendon Press, 1979).
48. M.N. Shaw, International Law, 3rd ed. (Cambridge: Grotius Publications Ltd., 1991), p. 243.
49. House of Lords Debates, vol. 48, April 1980, col. 1121. See also, C.R. Symmons, "United Kingdom Abolition of the Doctrine of Recognition of Governments: A Rose by Another Name?" 1981 Public Law, pp. 249–262.
50. US Department of State, Digest of US Practice in International Law 1977, p. 20.
51. Consider, for instance, the EC "Declaration on the Recognition of New States in Eastern Europe and in the Soviet Union" of 16 December 1991, which nowhere defines "state" but bases recognition on a kind of code of conduct for the new entities, including: respect for international agreements, protection of human rights and pacific settlement of

disputes. I am grateful to Robert McCorquodale of St. John's College, Cambridge, for providing me with this document.

52. Trial of German Major War Criminals, (London: H.M.S.O., 1946–51), pp. 99 and 155.

53. See the Charter of the International Military Tribunal annexed to the London Agreement of 8 August 1945, providing for the prosecution and punishment of major war criminals. Cited in Shaw, International, p. 180.

54. For a personal account of this, see John P. Humphrey, Human Rights & the United Nations: a great adventure (Dobbs Ferry, NY: Transnational Publishers, Inc., 1984), p. 15 and generally. UNGA Res. 95(1) of 11 December 1946 affirmed "the principles of international law as recognized by the Charter of the Nuremberg Tribunal and the judgement of the Tribunal."

55. Jarat Chopra, "Collective Enforcement of International Criminal Law," in Andy Knight, ed., *United Nations Reform Issues in the 1990s and Beyond* (forthcoming).

56. H. Lauterpacht, International Law and Human Rights (London: Stevens & Sons Ltd., 1950), p. 70.

57. Allott, Eunomia, para. 15.66 and 15.68.

58. Article 3, Universal Declaration of Human Rights 1948.

59. See further, James Crawford, ed., The Rights of Peoples (Oxford: Clarendon Press, 1988). The first generation was civil and political rights and the second social and economic rights.

60. The Legal Consequences for States of the Continued Presence of South Africa in Namibia (South West Africa) notwithstanding Security Council Resolution 276 (1970), Advisory Opinion I.C.J. Reports 1971, p. 31; Western Sahara Case, Advisory Opinion I.C.J. Reports 1975, para. 54–59. See also "Declaration on the Granting of Independence to Colonial Territories and Peoples," G.A. Resolution 1514 (XV) of 14 December 1960. Cf. Jarat Chopra, "Statement Regarding the Issue of the Western Sahara before the Fourth Committee of the United Nations General Assembly, 19 October 1992," UN Doc. A/C.4/47/2/Add. 3.

61. "Desiring . . . to ensure the exercise of the right of self-determination of the Cambodian people through free and fair elections," Agreement on a Comprehensive Political Settlement of the Cambodia Conflict, 23 October 1991. UN Doc. S/23177, annex, sect. II.

62. See further, Robert McCorquodale, "Self-Determination Beyond the Colonial Context and its Potential Impact on Africa," 4 African Journal of International Law (RADIC), Pt. 3, October 1992.

63. See further, Lea Brilmayer, "Secession and Self-Determination: A Territorial Interpretation," 16 Yale Journal of International Law 1991, p. 177.

64. BBC discussion cited in Madelaine Drohan, "So Long, Sovereignty: The blurring of borders," The Globe and Mail, 11 April 1992.
65. F.H. Hinsley, Power and the Pursuit of Peace (Cambridge: Cambridge University Press, 1963), p. 283.
66. Paul Lewis, "U.N. Chief Wants Troops in Yugoslavia Until Accord," New York Times, 18 February 1992.
67. At the opening session of the Committee of 34 deliberations on 19 April 1993, statements by Kofi Annan, UN Under-Secretary-General for Peacekeeping, and Louise Frachet, Canada's Permanent Representative to the UN, affirmed that UN operations have moved beyond the luxury of consent and that UN operations must be prepared for this contingency. Cf. Thomas G. Weiss and Jarat Chopra, "UN Should Enforce Peace," *Christian Science Monitor*, 2 February 1993.
68. UN Doc. A/43/629, Annex (1988). Italics added. This has been formally proposed in the "Report of the Secretary-General pursuant to the statement adopted by the Summit Meeting of the Security Council on 31 January 1992" entitled "An Agenda for Peace: Preventive diplomacy, peacemaking and peace-keeping," UN Doc. A/47/277, S/24111 of 17 June 1992, para. 32. Cf. the UN deployment in Macedonia.
69. D.W. Bowett, United Nations Forces (London: Stevens & Sons, 1964), ch. 12.
70. Reparation for Injuries Suffered in the Service of the United Nations Case. Advisory Opinion, I.C.J. Reports 1949, p. 174. See further on implied powers, Certain Expenses of the United Nations Case. I.C.J. Reports 1962, p. 151.
71. Rahmatullah Khan, Implied Powers of the United Nations (New Delhi: Vikas Publications, 1970), p. 72.
72. John H. Halderman, "Legal Basis for United Nations Armed Forces," 56 American Journal of International Law 1962, pp. 972–973.
73. Bowett, Forces, p. 423; Doswald-Beck, "Invitation," p. 247.
74. See further, John Mackinlay and Jarat Chopra, "Second Generation Multinational Operations," The Washington Quarterly, vol. 15, no. 3, Summer 1992, pp. 113–131; A Draft Concept of Second Generation Multinational Operations 1993 (Providence, RI: Thomas J. Watson Jr. Institute for International Studies, 1993).
75. See further, Thomas G. Weiss and Jarat Chopra, United Nations Peacekeeping: An ACUNS Teaching Text (Hanover, NH: Academic Council on the United Nations System, 1992–1). On the UN Secretary-General's proposals for reform, see "An Agenda for Peace," UN Doc. A/47/277, S/24111; and Thomas G. Weiss, "New Challenges for UN Military Operations: Implementing an Agenda for Peace," *The Washington Quarterly*, Winter 1993, pp. 51–66.

Chapter 3

Sovereignty and Intervention

The Perspective for the Developing World

George Joffe

"International law is too fragile and too dependent on consensus and the example set by one of the world's most advanced societies not to suffer from the disregard and manipulation that recent US actions have inflicted on it."[1]

"Because each country has different national character-istics, there are varying perceptions and practices with regard to human rights ... The main responsibility for protecting human rights rests with governments. The principle of non-interference in the internal affairs of other nations is applicable to the question of human rights ... The importance of the relationship between collective human rights and world peace and development must be emphasized."[2]

In view of the growth in the global frequency of military intervention by major powers in the developed world since the late 1980s, it might seem surprising that states in the periphery[3] should perceive their problems of dealing with the core states of the West in wider terms. In fact, they do. Despite the attention given in the world's media to dramatic confrontations – such as that between the US-led and UN-authorized Multinational

Coalition and Iraq over the latter's annexation of Kuwait in 1990–91 or the US intervention in Panama in 1989 or, most recently, the sanctions imposed on Libya because of allegations over the Qadhdhafi regime's involvement in the destruction of Pan Am Flight No. 103 over Lockerbie in December 1988 – their immediate concerns are focused much more directly on economic intervention.

Their anxiety is particularly directed on programmes for economic restructuring as practised by the International Monetary Fund (IMF) and the International Bank for Reconstruction and Development (IBRD-World Bank). Both multilateral organizations form the core economic institutions set up at the Bretton Woods conference in the late 1940s and today their philosophies reflect the neoclassical economic concerns of the major powers, particularly the USA, rather than the Keynesian ideals of that period. Together with the General Agreement on Tariffs and Trade (GATT), they provide an ideological counterweight to the various economic institutions of the United Nations, particularly over the issue of economic development in the developing world (the periphery).

These wider concerns amongst peripheral states do not arise just because of the growing consensus amongst core states that the preferred mode of internal organization of the state should be focused around liberal democracies with free market economies. The concerns exist really because so much of the economic discourse between core and periphery today is formulated within the context of "conditionality"; that economic assistance is available only if recipient states conform to norms of democratic political behaviour and respect for human rights defined by the state or institution providing the assistance in question.

For the developing world of the periphery, therefore, the issue of intervention is global in its implications, touching not just on the threat of actual physical intervention but on every aspect of the tradition of the absolute sovereignty of the state, particularly as conventionally expressed in public international law. Not surprisingly, there is growing resentment over these pressures within peripheral states. This has developed not just amongst governments with unsavoury diplomatic and ethical records who might wish to use such an excuse to conceal their behaviour, but also amongst intellectuals and the wider public sphere in the developing world.

Military Intervention

At the same time, it is obvious that the most immediate concern, particularly in the Middle East and Central America, is the possibility of military intervention, not least because both areas have uncomfortable memories of recent experiences of this kind. The Middle East has had to confront the American-led Multinational Force in Beirut in 1982–83; the frequent clashes between the US Sixth Fleet and Libyan forces over access to the Gulf of Sirt in August 1981, in March 1986 and in January 1989, as well as the US bombing raids on Tripoli and Benghazi in April 1986; US naval action in the Gulf in 1987–88; and, finally, the Multinational Coalition against Iraq in 1990–91, with the later Operation "Safe Havens" and Operation "Provide Comfort" policies in Iraqi Kurdistan in mid-1991, as well as the creation of a new no-fly zone in southern Iraq during 1992, ostensibly to protect the Shi'a and Marsh Arab communities there from extinction.

Central America has had a long history of American intervention under the "Monroe Doctrine" and the "Roosevelt Corollary". Whereas the "Monroe Doctrine" legitimized exclusive American rights to unilateral intervention in Central American affairs, the "Roosevelt Corollary" refined this by permitting such intervention in neighbouring republics, ". . . to prevent chronic wrongdoing," and was first enunciated by President Theodore Roosevelt in 1904. There were seven interventions in Central America between 1903 and 1920 and three more in the 1920s, until the "Roosevelt Corollary" was formally abandoned in 1930 by Secretary-of-State Henry Stimson. The frequency of such events then declined. However, the interventionist policies of the Reagan and Bush administrations – in Grenada and Panama, at least – really represent a revival of the Corollary[4]. Nor should the British intervention to reverse Argentina's occupation of the Falklands-Malvinas Islands in 1982 be forgotten, particularly since it was the first major incident of the present sequence of interventions.

The most striking example of such intervention, of course, has been the Multinational Coalition's intervention against Iraq in 1990–91. The predominant concern in the Middle East over this intervention was not whether or not Iraq's annextaion of Kuwait could be tolerated. Most responsible Middle Eastern opinion agreed that Iraq's actions could not be allowed to stand. The real problem was the way in which it was to be reversed – by a Western military intervention – and, of course, over the extraordinary distinction between the immediacy of Western concern over Kuwait and Iraq's breach of international norms, as opposed to the lack of interest and response manifested by Western states over Israel's behaviour, particularly in the Occupied Territories, over many decades.

Behind this resentment at the differential treatment being meted out by the major core powers, there is a very real concern which was typified by the attitude adopted towards Libya in late 1991 and during 1992, which was designed to force the Qadhdhafi regime to hand over two Libyans accused of complicity in the bombings of airliners and to renounce all support for international terrorism. The issue here was not the actual facts of the case – whether the evidence connecting those Libyans accused by Britain, the USA and France of being involved in the destruction of Pan Am Flight PA 103 over Lockerbie in December 1988 or in the destruction of the UTA flight over Niger in September 1989 was correct or not – but the way in which those claims have been manipulated to create an *a priori* basis for accusing the Libyan government and its leader, Colonel Mu^{c}ammar Qadhdhafi, of being responsible for what happened. Official Libyan resentment at the behaviour of the UN Security Council is well caught by an article in *Le Monde* of April 8, 1992, by the Libyan premier, Abuzayid Umar Durda, entitled "Complot contre la Libye". The article begins:–

"L'injustice et l'arbitraire seraient-ils, en définitive, les seuls ressorts de ce 'nouvel order international' que les Etat-Unis, libres, désormais, de gouverner à leur guise les affaires du monde, entreprennent d'instituer depuis près de deux ans?"

Nonetheless, many, both in Libya and in the wider developing world, would answer in the affirmative to his rhetorical question – as, indeed, not surprisingly he did himself! In effect, many in the developing world, particularly in the Arab world, feel that the United Nations Security Council has been manipulated by the three permanent members concerned - France, Britain and the USA – to act as their agent in coercing Libya, whatever the merits of the case. Even worse, in their view, was the fact that virtually all other states in the core developed world and many states in the periphery colluded in such behaviour, largely, they suspected, from fear than from conviction.

In short, the fundamental assumptions of public international law and the basic principles of the United Nations have been distorted to achieve objectives established by major Western powers as part of their vision of the New World Order. Many people, not just in the Middle East nor, indeed, only in the developing world but also in the developed world, believe that Western aggressiveness towards Libya is merely the first stage in imposing a Western vision of appropriate international conduct on states worldwide. After Libya, they expect Syria or perhaps Lebanon to be pilloried for their sponsorship for state terrorism and, after them, Iran.

The major difference between these two groups, however, is not over the scenario they envisage but over its justifiability. For the majority of those in the West, such an attitude is justifiable in the interests of crushing terrorism, whatever its cause or stimulus. For the developing world, it is not because it smacks increasingly of Western imperiousness and imposition, of a neo-colonial approach to international relations reminiscent far more of the gunboat diplomacy of the nineteenth century than of a world controlled by universally accepted legal principle for the New World Order of the twenty first century. This latter view was the concept first formulated, after all, by President Bush in an address to a joint session of Congress in September 1990 when he said:–

"Out of these troubled times, our fifth objective – a new world order – can emerge; a new era – freer from the threat of terror, stronger in the pursuit of justice, and more secure in the quest for peace, an era in which the nations of the world, East and west, North and South, can prosper and live in harmony."

The tragedy is that the practice and threat of military intervention by the USA, buttressed by Britain and France, seem, to most observers in the developing world of the periphery, to directly contradict that aspiration.

Intervention, the basic legal principles

Behind these contradictory views, there is a very real dilemma which was well summed up by Professor Adam Roberts on May 8, 1991, in the annual Martin Wright Memorial Lecture:—

"International law and society are still caught propounding contradictory principles: on the one hand, the sovereignty of states and non-intervention in their internal affairs, and on the other hand human rights; on the one hand the equality of states, and on the other the special privileges of the five permanent members of the UN Security Council ... Power is still the key factor in international relations — even if it is more ambiguous in its character, more varied in its forms, and less of an over-arching goal which can be single-mindedly pursued without reference to other considerations, than some of the so-called 'realists' implied."[5]

Of course, people in the developing world would argue that it is precisely because power *can* now be wielded without ambiguity that the New World Order is, for them, a betrayal. In any case, it is the issue of international law which is the primary concern to most commentators in the developing world and, conventionally, it is the United Nations which is claimed to be the embodiment of the international legal system. It is, after all, an international regime that seeks to avoid conflict between states and to regulate the types of behaviour in which states may legitimately engage. That was, indeed, the formal rationale for its creation in the aftermath of the destruction wrought by the Second World War.

For states on the periphery of the international community, however, it is now not clear that, in practice, this is really how the United Nations now operates or, indeed, will operate in the future. Ironically enough, it could be argued that, with the end of the Cold War, the United Nations is now acting as its founders intended, as a vehicle of the wishes of the five permanent members, given their veto power within the Security Council. In this case, the idea that the United Nations is a forum for a community of nations, all of equal power and status, is in their eyes clearly a misreading of the UN Charter.

Nonetheless, international law is clearly their primordial concern for it is the only guarantee they have against the unrestrained use of force in international affairs. What, then, is the status of public customary international law and of the United Nations Charter over the issue of military intervention and to what extent do states in the periphery subscribe to it? The basic issue is the status of the state in international law and the degree to which this has been modified by the United Nations Charter. Allied to this is the status of rights of intervention in states under international law and the extent to which these rights have been modified by recent concerns with human rights and the role of multilateral organizations.

The state is the primordial legal personality in international law.[6] States express this by their right to absolute sovereignty over their territories and their governments merely have to ensure that they are independent of any other authority and that they enjoy legislative and administrative competence to be recognized as the legitimate controlling authority of the state. In other words they do not have to be "democratic" in any sense of the word to qualify as legitimate governments. In their relations with other states, states are all assumed to be of equal status, as an extension of the concept of absolute state sovereignty; thus no state can dictate, in terms of international law, at least, the behaviour of one of its fellows, unless there is a general agreement that states should derogate a degree of sovereign decision to some other body.

It is at this point that international and multilateral bodies acquire a specific significance in international law, for they are precisely those bodies to which, by agreement, member-states have ceded a degree of sovereign decision. It is important to realize that, in public international law, these international bodies such as the United Nations and the European Community, not to speak of bodies such as the IMF and the World Bank, may well have international legal personalities and thus be able to enter into discourse and agreements with states, but they do not have a superior legal status to their member-states. Indeed, the United Nations does have a legal personality, but, as the International Court of Justice argued in the Corfu Channel Case [7]neither it nor its member-states have an inherent right of intervention against other states.[8]

There are, however, certain circumstances in which state sovereignty is limited and rights of intervention do exist. States are normally immune from legal restraint in their relations with other states, for they have sovereign immunity. This, however, today is normally interpreted to apply only to governmental acts by the state (acts *iure imperii*) and not to its commercial acts (acts *iure gestionis*) or to such acts carried out by its representatives. States thus have qualified sovereign immunity, a situation accepted by the USA in 1952 and by Britain in 1978[9]. In addition, this restriction only applies to actions by a particular state within another state and not to the overall corpus of its diplomatic acts. The basic assumption of absolute state sovereignty is thus preserved. In fact, suggestions that these and other restrictions on sovereignty undermine the very nature of the concept[10] overlook the crucial distinction that they result from voluntary derogation by the state concerned. The state may, therefore, withdraw such derogation if it wishes.

Thus, states may agree within multilateral organizations to derogate a portion of their absolute sovereignty. They do this as members of the United Nations, for example, by subscribing to the United Nations Charter. Once again, the fact that this is a voluntary gesture which can, in theory, be withdrawn counters the argument that there is an inherent contradiction between the concepts of international law and sovereignty. Sovereignty remains the property of the state and the definition of its mode of domestic control, akin to Weber's view of the state as the entity with the domestic monopoly over the use of legitimate violence. International law consists of the voluntarily accepted principles regulating state behaviour amongst the community of states[11].

The most important element that is sacrificed within international law is the unrestrained right to use force to further the objectives of the state in question. In fact, this limitation on the sovereign power of states goes back to the original Covenant of the League of Nations, signed in 1919, and the Kellogg-Briand Pact, signed by 63 nations in 1928. The first required that the territorial integrity of member-states should be respected and the second outlawed the use of force by sovereign states except in self-defence. They have been incorporated into international law and thus, since the end of the First World War, the use of force by states has been severely curtailed – in legal terms, at least[12]. Now, however, both have been superseded by Article 2(4) of the United Nations Charter, which states that:–

> "All members shall refrain in their international relations from the threat or use of force against the territorial integrity or political independence of any state, or in any manner inconsistent with the Purposes of the United Nations."

This article, however, does raise the possibility that there are occasions when the use of force would be consistent with the "Purposes of the United Nations". The purposes are delimited in Article 1 of the Charter as "To maintain international peace and security" through measures involving " . . . peaceful means and in conformity with the principles of justice and international law." It is generally considered by international lawyers that this formulation means that the use of force is now prohibited by international law, except in certain well-defined circumstances, as provided for in the United Nations Charter. These are for the purpose of:–

(1) Self-defence, whether by individual or a collective regional security organization (Article 51);

(2) Collective measures authorized by the United Nations (Article 42), although recourse to force may only take place once "peaceful means" have failed (Article 33), the peaceful means including sanctions (Article 41); and

(3) When authorized by the competent United Nations body (the Security Council) but only under the terms of Article 42

which allows the Security Council to delegate its authority to a state or group of states.

Interestingly enough, certain specific situations are considered to fall outside these exceptions to the use of force. It is not necessarily legal under the Charter or under customary public international law for a state to intervene in another state to protect nationals of the first state. Nor, indeed, is forceful intervention for humanitarian purposes necessarily *a priori* a legal act under international law, although, under the "Universality Principle" certain acts by individuals are construed to be international crimes over which any state may exercise jurisdiction[13]. Interestingly enough, such crimes involve piracy, genocide, war crimes and aircraft hijacking but not international terrorism. The principle applies to forceful intervention in a situation of civil war[14].

It should also be noted, of course, that, since the United Nations Security Council is the appropriate forum in which these matters are decided, the veto power of the permanent five members ensures that the real power of decision-making devolves upon them, provided that their affirmative vote for any action is supported by four other Council member-states. The point here is that the terms of Article 27, which governs voting procedures in the Security Council, allows any one of the five permanent members to block Security Council action by refusing an affirmative vote but requires an absolute majority of nine votes in the Council – including, obviously, all five permanent members – for any action they collectively wish to encourage to be adopted by the Security Council; hence the endless lobbying and arm-twisting, particularly of developing world member-states of the Council, over particularly important votes.

It is this voting power of the five permanent members that states in the periphery particularly dislike because it has two consequences which they see as adverse. Firstly, their views can simply be blocked by any one permanent member, thus giving the developed world core a predominant role inside the United Nations and thereby destroying the presupposition of the equality of states in international law. Secondly, it encourages a considerable degree of coercion on non-permanent member-states of the Security Council if the five permanent members wish to see a particular course of action undertaken – which also violates the same presupposition of state equality.

Yet, of course, this was precisely the way the United Nations was originally intended to act, for the "Big Five" at the end of the Second World War were determined to create an organization that would not suffer from the ineffectiveness of the old League of Nations and that would articulate their collective vision of what the postwar world order should be. It was only the Cold War which prevented this vision from becoming reality and, thereby, gave the rapidly expanding developing world of the 1950s, 1960s and 1970s a degree of unexpected freedom of diplomatic action. Now, however, with the end of the Cold War, the original assumptions behind the United Nations have been reinstated and the developing world is coming to terms with the fact that it is not an organization that is inherently amicable to the interests of the periphery or to the way in which the periphery perceives its interests to be formulated.

The post-Cold War reality

The basic problem is that, for states in the developing world, both the existence of the veto power for the five permanent members of the Security Council and the fact of their permanent presence on the Security Council contradict the fundamental assumption of the equality of states within the context of international law. This was a tolerable situation during the Cold War because the antagonism between Western and Eastern permanent members meant that the veto power nullified their built-in advantages and an effective balance of power was established within the organization which peripheral states could exploit. In addition, within the General Assembly, the developing world managed to maintain a dominance and an ability, thereby, to influence the general tenor of United Nations policy – although the only executive power held by the Assembly is to approve the United Nations budget, to assess financial contributions from member-states and to elect the Secretary-General and other senior officials.

All this has now gone, for, with the end of the Cold War, the balance of power inside the United Nations has disappeared and the dominant role of the five permanent members, particularly of the Western members, has been reasserted. As a result, actions such as the United Nations Security Council-authorized delegation of authority to the USA and its partners in the Multinational Coalition against Iraq and the current Security Council sanctions against Libya – both at the behest of the dominant Western members of the permanent members group – have become possible.

This new activism within the United Nations, which seems to periphery states to be primarily directed against them, is mirrored in the wider world as well. Indeed, during the 1980s, military interventions have been carried out primarily by two states – the USA and Britain – and have reflected the growing detente between the USA and the former Soviet Union. France has also engaged in a series of interventions in Africa, albeit as part of its traditional neo-patriarchalism towards its former West African and Central African colonies.

Now that the antagonistic balance of power between the two former superpowers has come to an end, there appears to be no restraint on potential Western interventionism as the legal assumptions over sovereign immunity and equality are replaced by an aggressive Western view of *realpolitik*. Whether or not this is an objective analysis of the current situation, it is certainly how it appears to the developing world.

Furthermore, this growing readiness to practise military intervention is partnered by a more long standing determination to intervene in social and economic spheres – an issue that goes back to the start of the 1980s and the growth of the foreign debt crisis in the developing world after the first oil price crisis of 1973–74 and the second oil price crisis in 1979–80.

In this respect, the IMF and the World Bank, which are seen by periphery states as Western-dominated institutions, have led the way in interventionism and in the destruction of the basic legal assumption of absolute state sovereignty. Nor is this interventionist attitude particularly covert. With the growing integration of the world economy and global trading patterns, there is a considerable body of opinion within the states of the developed core which argues that their governments have a right to protect their national economic and political interests within this integrated structure by some form of intervention, if necessary.

Recognizing this danger, American leaders have developed a comprehensive method for dealing with anti-systemic crises: low-intensity conflict strategy. The authors of *Discriminate Deterrence* argue that LIC capacity is vital, since

"... if we do not improve our ability to counter this lesser threat, we will surely lose the support of many Third World countries that want to believe the United States can protect its friends, not to mention its own interests. Violence in the Third World threatens our interests in a variety of ways."

In a report to Congress in 1984, Secretary of Defense Weinberger argued: "Our economies (advanced capitalist) and the economies of our allies (Third World) are, therefore, especially susceptible to disruption from conflicts far from our own borders". Military planners have also recognized this connection between rapid socioeconomic change produced by third world industrialization and the grave conflict situations which might have to be confronted by the new LIC strategy. Retired US Army General Paul Gorman has also stressed the global economic transformation outlined in this paper as a primary cause of 'strategic challenges' that demand the kind of US response outlined by LIC doctrine.[15]

Statements such as these must make the blood of the developing world's politicians run cold, for they are directly opposed to traditional assumptions about the inviolability of state sovereignty. Peripheral states, in short, must expect and accept economic interventionism through the IMF and World Bank and politico-military interventionism, either via the United Nations – long seen as the guarantor of their inviolability but now subordinated to the political objectives of the developed world – or directly by powerful states in the core of the new world system.

Indeed, they actually face a new systemic approach towards the concept of sovereignty which undermines all the old certitudes. Here the willingness of independent sovereign states to coalesce into multilateral organizations to ensure global economic and political order has been replaced by the hegemonic dominance of one state (the USA) or group of states (the West) which subverts the multilateralism of the past in its own interests, thus achieving the role of 'hegemonic stability' so beloved of Cold War strategists[16]. The fact that the USA may not be able to maintain its dominant economic hegemony is of minor significance, if that burden can be accepted by other core actors, such as the EC or even Japan. The fundamental new world order remains, unless new forms of multilateralism can be created to replace it[17]. Nor does the attack on the old assumptions of the developing world periphery over sovereignty end there, for there are now two new arenas in which they are threatened.

One is over environmental control, where multilateral organizations will be essential to deal with ecological and environmental problems that extend beyond the boundaries and capacities of a single state. Indeed, here periphery states may be very willing to agree to such limitations on their sovereignty, provided that their own economic development is not hindered – the cases of the Brazilian rain-forests and of hydro-electrical power generation in Czechoslovakia, Hungary or China come to mind, as does that of the most acute current problem, the issue of fluoro-hydrocarbons and the ozone layer. They would also be prepared to cooperate more willingly if states within the core were also prepared to make the same sovereign sacrifices, particularly over issues such as atmospheric pollution for which the developed world is primarily responsible – something which the USA, for one, is singularly unwilling to do. Periphery states, therefore, tend to react negatively to such proposals of reductions in sovereign control, however desirable they might objectively be.

It has recently been argued that state boundaries ignore biome boundaries – boundaries around natural eco-regions – and this contradiction can be a source of conflict. The argument also suggests that the full potential of biomes can only be realized by the cessation of a degree of state sovereignty in place of regional or multilateral cooperation, particularly through the principle of 'subsidarity', whereby local ecological management should become the rule with sovereign entities, such as states, only intervening when local entities no longer have the necessary confidence or competence. This concept of 'subsidarity' is already applied to environmental issues within the European Communities.[18].

Unfortunately, the core states of the developed world are very unwilling to cooperate in such developments, as they made abundantly clear at the United Nations "Earth Summit" environmental conference in Rio de Janeiro during June 1992. Although agreements were signed there, major states in the developed world ensured that their enforcement criteria were rendered ineffective and, in one case, the United States simply refused to sign the treaty at all. Interestingly enough, President Bush's reasons were that he would not tolerate signatories to such treaty in the periphery being able to threaten US economic activity – in other words, the president was not prepared to consent to a limitation of any kind on American sovereignty! Not surprisingly, this reluctance, in turn, has sadly provided plenty of justification for similar reluctance to make the necessary sacrifices amongst the states of the periphery.

The other proposed modification of sovereignty is far more immediately serious for the developing world. This is that sovereignty is no longer a property of the state but of a 'people', in the sense in which the term is used in the United Nations Charter. In effect, the term is synonymous with the concept of a 'nation' and, as a result, governments only have sovereign power if they are legitimized through popular support, not because, as in the past, of their independence or their administrative and legislative competence. Democratic consent thus becomes an essential component of state sovereignty.

There are four basic texts on which this view is based: the American constitution; the Declaration of the Rights of Man during the French Revolution; the United Nations Charter; and the Universal Declaration of Human Rights, now considered to have declaratory status under customary international law and which affirms that:–

"The will of the people shall be the basis for the authority of government; this will shall be expressed in periodic and genuine elections which shall be by universal and equal suffrage and shall be held by secret vote or by equivalent free voting procedures."

Legal authorities are now beginning to imitate their political counterparts in arguing that this justifies humanitarian military intervention, either through LIC or by direct foreign intervention, whatever traditional concepts of sovereignty might have been[19]. It is little wonder that states in the periphery, whatever their political systems, see this as a further threat to their autonomy and sovereign existence.

Nor are they alone in this quandary, for international relations theorists are by no means certain that sovereignty is necessarily only legitimized by popular consent to government. Sovereignty, it has been argued, means "constitutional independence" in a world where all states are of "equal status".[20] Intervention, then, is generally impermissible, for states may legitimately pursue their own independent internal policies. Humanitarian interventions, in particular, would be impermissible in this context, irrespective of whether the state were a *machtstaat* or a *rechtstaat*.

On the other hand, arguments based in semiotics suggest that state sovereignty has no meaning except when it is confronted by the possibility of intervention. Indeed, sovereign statehood itself can only be given substance insofar as the state can embody the popular authority of its citizens which, at the same time, it thereby symbolizes. In this definition of sovereignty, it is the fact that the state is at the same time the expression and the symbol of the authority of a defined and unique community which renders intervention impermissible within an international regime. If, however, sovereignty does not have this meaning, then the state itself is delegitimized and intervention is a legitimate activity simply because the supposedly sovereign state is not an expression or a symbol of the general will[21]. The fact that the domestic community had withdrawn its consent for the state to symbolize it would make humanitarian intervention not only permissible but also desirable because the state itself has lost real meaning and can no longer participate in an international regime in which other states continue to retain their legitimacy and significance.

Legitimate intervention

In any case, there are opportunities at present, under international law at least, for military intervention. They are, however, still very restricted unless the five permanent members are prepared to abuse their veto power inside the United Nations Security Council. This, certainly, is the general view in the developing world and explains the growing resentment voiced at both government and popular levels with Security Council's activities in recent months; indeed, ever since the second Gulf war. This resentment supplements the anger in the developing world that originally developed over unilateral interventions in the Middle East, Central America and Latin America during the 1980s. Quite apart from the popular realization that states in the developing world had unilaterally – whether individually or through the agency of the United Nations Security Council – decided to intervene militarily, there were considerable anxieties over the international legal propriety of the ways in which these interventions had been organized and justified.

 The American decision to penetrate the Gulf of Sirt in 1982 and 1986, for example, was justified on the ground that these waters were 'high seas' and thus international in scope, despite a Libyan declaration in 1973 which had legalized their transformation into Libyan internal waters on the grounds of historic title and security. The USA disputed the closure declaration under customary international law, arguing that the Gulf of Sirt was too large to qualify as a bay. Yet, the USA, Italy and the former Soviet Union all have declared bays and gulfs of similar dimensions (Chesapeake Bay, the Gulf of Taranto and St. Peter-the-Great Bay respectively) closed internal waters on precisely the same grounds of security[22]. The US bombing of Libyan cities in April 1986 was justified under Article 51 of the United Nations Charter whereby the USA invoked the right of self-defence against supposed Libyan terrorism in Berlin – a claim that was widely felt to have been an unreasonable extension of the meaning of the article in question, quite apart from the fact that there has since been considerable doubt thrown on its veracity.

The same justification was used by the USA before the Security Council to justify its intervention in Panama in December 1989, although President Bush had cited four different grounds for the invasion decision just after it took place. These were, 1) to protect American lives, 2) to apprehend General Noriega for "narco-crime" and bring him to trial, 3) to restore democracy to Panama and 4) to "ensure the integrity of the Canal Treaties"[23]. However, since no state of war existed either prior to or after the invasion (US diplomats used the fiction that the USA had been 'invited' into Panama by the Endara government), military intervention to protect American lives was illegal. In any case, the intervention ran counter to the United Nations Charter and the Charter of the Organization of American States. Furthermore, the Canal Treaties do not permit military intervention and the extension of US municipal law – General Noriega had been indicted of drugs offenses within the USA – through military intervention has no standing in international law, any more than does the decision to "restore democracy"[24].

It should be pointed out that this interpretation was not universally accepted by American lawyers. Nonetheless, one typical legal argument in favour of the president's position justified the invasion on humanitarian grounds. These were that it was directed against a tyrannical and dictatorial government, in which President Bush was acting in the humanitarian tradition first established by Britain, France and Russia when they intervened in the Turko-Greek war of 1827 to protect Christians[25].

The most serious doubts, however, have been raised over the legal status of the United Nations-authorized intervention against Iraq in 1990–91 and the imposition of sanctions against Libya. In the case of the Multinational Coalition against Iraq numerous objections have been raised, from the failure of the United Nations Security Council to fully exhaust peaceful means of settling the dispute before turning to military action, as required by Articles 33 and 42 of the United Nations Charter, to the failure to consult the Military Staff Committee as required by Article 47 and failing to establish its own military plans as required by Article 46[26]. The only basis for the actual pattern of action undertaken seems to reside in Article 53, whereby the Security Council may utilize ". . . regional arrangements or agencies for enforcement action under its authority". However, in the eyes of many governments in the developing world, the Multinational Coalition was a violation of the United Nations Charter and the most blatant example to date of the use of the United Nations as an agent of 'hegemonic stability' controlled by the USA.

The issue of sanctions against Libya because of its supposed sponsorship of international terrorism, to whit the destruction of a Pan Am flight over Lockerbie in 1988 and the destruction of a UTA flight over Niger in 1989, seemed to have even less justification under the United Nations Charter or under public international law. First of all, there was no evidence cited to demonstrate that the Libyan government was actually implicated in the incidents, even if some of its citizens were. Secondly, there was evidence that nationals of other states and even the governments of those states themselves were involved, evidence which has so far been ignored by the United Nations Security Council. Thirdly, the sanctions decision can only by the greatest stretch of the imagination be construed to fall under Article 51 of the Charter and there is no customary international law that construes terrorism to be *a priori* an international crime. States in the developing world, therefore, are drawn to the inevitable conclusion that, once more, the United Nations is being forced to act as the agent of three of the five permanent members of the Security Council and that the United Nations itself is apparently prepared to abandon fundamental principles of international law and the absolute nature of the sovereignty of the state.

Nonetheless, the current changes in the international climate may legitimately require a reconsideration of the traditional view of the universal and absolute sovereignty of states, for the reality of world order at present could be described as:–

". . . the European world, the world of the Paris Charter of 1990, is a Grotian one, observing norms of cooperation, and perhaps even has its Kantian element: a civil society of civil societies, with sovereignty fraying at the edges; while at least parts of the world beyond are still Hobbesian, with

force still a very active final arbiter within and between countries, and sovereignty loudly proclaimed."[27]
This, however, still does not legitimize the right of those states within the "civil society of civil societies" to intervene in the Hobbesian periphery. The principle of non-intervention remains the same, for it is still the basis of the current international regime – or so states in the periphery believe.

In fact, as described above, the issue has now become a major concern of commentators in international relations as well as to politicians in the developed world[28]. Quite apart from the arguments derived from semiology discussed there, it has also been argued that, since institutions such as the Conference on Security and Cooperation in Europe (CSCE), for example, can become a "Wertegemeinschaft", violations of human and minority rights are a collective interest which permits external pressures to be applied against offending regimes, thereby reducing the role of sovereign immunity of a state even further than the current doctrine of qualified immunity requires – although, in this case, within a framework of freely consenting states within the core.

In short, such a diminuition of sovereign immunity is only acceptable if states voluntarily accept that they should derogate some degree of their sovereign authority to other institutions. Indeed, this could be construed to be a characteristic of regional organizations, of which the European Community is the best-known example. Others where there are security implications which hamper the freedom of action of individual member-states – which have thus derogated a degree of their sovereign power – are the *Gulf Cooperation Council* (GCC) and the *Maghreb Arab Union* (UMA).

The classic moral position was described by John Stuart Mill in 1867:–

"A civilized government cannot help having barbarous neighbours: when it has, it cannot always content itself with a defensive position, one of mere resistance to aggression. After a longer or a shorter interval of forbearance, it either finds itself obliged to conquer them, or to assert so much authority over them, and so break their spirit that they gradually sink into a state of dependence upon itself; and when that time arrives, they are indeed no longer formidable to it, but it has had so much to do with setting up and putting down their governments, and they have grown so accustomed to lean on it, that it has become morally responsible for all evil it allows them to do."[29]

However, this moral attitude does not fit within the context of public international law, even if it reflects the concept of the state as a *rechtstaat* and appears similar to some theoretical interpretations of sovereignty and the sovereignty/intervention boundary. International law is certainly based on ethical principle but the ethics involved are juridical and intrinsic to the evolution of the system itself. It cannot, thereby, be obliged to justify actions within the international arena which reflect moral and ethical principles not inherent within its own juridical construct. Indeed:–

"Every ethical system must insist on the priority of its own principles, or else it undermines its claim to be an ethical system – a system entitled to guide and govern human conduct. Legal systems, too, must insist on the priority of their own principles, or else they surrender their authority and become simply one, possibly indispensable, means for achieving ends that are defined by some other ethical system. What holds true for law in general holds also for international law. As a normative system, international law is concerned with whether or not particular acts or policies are lawful, not whether they are desirable or morally justifiable. For international law to provide a consistent and authoritative way of dealing with the question of lawfulness, the answers it generates must derive from its own traditions and procedures and not from the arguments of moralists or philosophers."[30]

It is for this reason, no doubt, that the concept of "popular sovereignty" has not replaced "state sovereignty" and that international law still looks to governmental competence, rather than to democratic credentials in determining whether a government is legitimate or not. In short, legal precept does not automatically accord rights of intervention on humanitarian grounds or on the basis of the lack of democracy or respect for human rights manifested by a particular regime.

The reasons for this are partly pragmatic and partly historical. They derive from the evolution of international legal practice over minorities and "self-determination". Historically, the concept of "self-determination" as applied to national minorities proved extremely difficult to incorporate into the old League of Nations Covenant and did not survive into the United Nations Charter. Instead, the Charter referred only to "peoples" and subsequent acts of the United Nations General Assembly, particularly UNGA Resolution No. 1514 (XV) of December 1960, have made it clear that "people" to whom rights of self-determination apply are predominantly former colonial peoples[31], thus creating the so-called "salt water convention".

Pragmatically, states resist intervention – and the corpus of international law justifies them in such resistance – over questions of minority rights because of the attendant dangers of conflict and the fear of hegemony on the part of those who intervene. It is also the case that most states in the developed world, which are, in fact, multi-ethnic, maintain a fiction that their various ethnicities, or "peoples", have in the past voluntarily accepted the ethos of the state in which they live, so that issues of self-determination cannot apply to them[32]. This is a situation that is manifestly unjust to states in the periphery which are regularly subject to such pressures by their peers in the developed world, since it, once again, underlines the reality of perceptions of *inequality* in the interstate world order by member-states of the core.

In fact, the international legal situation is clear. It is that:–

"The interstate system is "a conservative order". It does not condone humanitarian intervention, since it does not define concern for human rights violations as a legitimate reason to intervene. Basically, intervention is condoned only if the state in question has requested it or has given its consent or if intervention is based on an IGO decision."[33]

Of course, the IGO (inter-governmental organization) can make such a decision because the state in question has voluntarily derogated a degree of national sovereignty in becoming a member and has, thereby, provided an implicit permission for such decisions to be made.

In short, the development of international legal principle, both in customary international law and in the United Nations as a source of declaratory international law, over national minorities and self-determination, provides a guide towards the general issue of rights of intervention over humanitarian issues in general, including minority rights, human rights and democratic rights. The general principle is that intervention is not permitted except in certain specified cases, namely, where states have explicitly or implicitly agreed that such intervention should occur and in the case of 'international crime', such as genocide. In effect, the essential elements of absolute state sovereignty and of the egalitarian nature of the global interstate system has been preserved within the international legal corpus.

Peripheral states, therefore, are quite within their rights to object to the attempts by states in the core to unilaterally intervene in their domestic affairs, whatever the moral justification, without their consent. Indeed, respect for this basic principle of state equality and state sovereignty should be an essential component of any "New World Order" that is now being created. If it is not, the unilateral procuration of rights of intervention by certain states, whatever the justification, will destroy the fragile structure through which states generally tacitly agree to cooperate within the interstate system.

Even though critics such as Michael Walzer have argued that rights of intervention do exist when "communal autonomy" – the right of contemporary men and women to live as members of a historic community and to express their inherited culture through political forms worked out among themselves – is threatened, they still agree that the general principle must be one of non-intervention. Even the more extreme 'reform interventionists' such as David Luban, who argue that military intervention is permissible if basic moral rights are infringed, do not argue that there is a duty of enforcement to intervene. Even when there is, Mapel argues that the danger of "collateral damage" to use a sinister term common during the second Gulf war, usually vitiates even this possibility. Rights of military intervention, even on humanitarian grounds, are thus extremely limited and only when a particular regime is demonstrably illegitimate – as manifest through universal dissent – could unilateral intervention be legally sanctioned without the prior consent of the state concerned[34].

Economic and social intervention

Intervention, however, is not merely military in nature. Indeed, as states have become increasingly integrated into the global economy in the past two decades, there has been a growing tendency for multilateral bodies, which usually articulate the economic interests and beliefs of states in the developed world, to intervene in the economic development of the developing world. The primary justification for this has been the problem of foreign debt, incurred usually as a result of either a "rush for development" based on borrowed funds for state investment, or as a result of loans acquired in the wake of the First and Second Oil Price Shocks of the 1973–74 and 1979–80 periods in order to cover the cost of imported energy. The generally adverse terms of international trade, coupled with a slow down in economic growth in the developing world, meant that many states were unable to meet repayment schedules and had, therefore, to turn to the IMF for help in balancing their external accounts and the World Bank for financial support in modernizing their economies.

The problem has been that all aid has been conditional on three separate conditions – economic liberalization and increased 'openness' of the economies in difficulties, and the political pre-condition of 'conditionality' – the requirement that the states concerned meet externally approved standards of human rights observance and democratic political structures before any of this aid is made available. The 'conditionality' principle is a relatively late addition to the purely economic requirements originally put in place by the IMF and the World Bank and reflects the growing confidence of Western leaders that the end of the Cold War permits them to impose such conditions without international hindrance. However, even the economic reform requirements involve a hidden political agenda, for they reflect the ideological victory of "neo-classical economics" over "Keynesian economics" since the mid-1970s in determining what economic orthodoxy should be. Each of these terms deserves, therefore, some attention, for each of them, in effect, impinges directly on the sovereignty of the state, particularly for states in the periphery[35].

Economic liberalization

Economic liberalization is considered vital by both the IMF and the World Bank because they also consider that difficulties over debt repayment reflect fundamental weaknesses in the economies of the states concerned and not any core changes in the external economic environment. The basic problem is the misallocation of resources through unrealistic pricing policies in the economy concerned[36]. The cure, then, for the inability to maintain debt repayment schedules, is to restore a proper allocation of resources within the economy and this requires the development of appropriate pricing structures. Fundamentally, economies must be converted to free market principles; state control of economic activity must be radically reduced by the removal of state subsidies and the privatization of state assets; fiscal, monetary and exchange rate policies must be adjusted to international norms and the trade regime must be oriented towards exports, whilst not restricting import penetration.

Such policies, of course, cause massive economic hardship and social discontent within the society concerned. They are thus a profound factor for political instability and consequent government repression, with all the attendant dangers of abuse of human rights and minority interests. They are often accompanied by or encourage harsh, undemocratic government, since this is the only way in which the reforms themselves can be pushed through and effective political control maintained. Furthermore, since they do not allow for the role of the external economic environment and often operate inside small economies, the net benefits in terms of foreign debt reduction are usually minimal – as the chronic debt crisis of Latin America and Africa make clear.

There is, however, another aspect which worsens the picture. This is that the fundamental objective of the reforms in question is to render the economies concerned more efficient so that the process of economic development and modernization will be accelerated. That, in itself, is a noble objective and should not cause any objection, for it should mark the transformation of the state from prebendalism towards economic structures capable of supporting effective civil societies and institutional forms that will eventually legitimize the state itself as a *rechtstaat*.

However, the technique proposed to achieve this transformation is completely experimental. No economy to date has achieved effective economic development successfully in this way. The economies of the developed world grew slowly and usually enjoyed considerable economic protection, if not privileged access to wider markets. The so-called 'Tiger' economies of South-East Asia developed behind protectionist barriers and often in conjunction with specific multinational corporation investment. They also generally enjoyed a partnership between state and private sector that is not permitted under current IMF and World Bank orthodoxies. In short, the type of economic development forced upon peripheral economies actually worsens the conditions under which economic development can successfully occur. Ironically enough, it is now the former socialist regimes of Eastern Europe and the Commonwealth of Independent States which have become the latest proving ground for these experimental procedures -just at a time when the World Bank, if not the IMF, is beginning to question their efficacy.

Openness

'Openness' is allied to economic liberalization and is the concept that, through the reduction of barriers to international trade and "the free flow of goods, capital, people and knowledge"[37], economic development will benefit. However, in the short term, liberalization of trade regimes tends to result in a worsening of the trade balance and concomitant monetary and fiscal restraint to compress domestic demand so that the balance can be restored. It does not dramatically improve export performance because most peripheral economies suffer from adverse terms of trade for their primary product exports.

87

This can only change if they develop adequate export-oriented industrial sectors and can penetrate the vast markets of the developed world, such as the EC, the USA and Japan.

For this to be achieved, the countries concerned need massive amounts of investment. In effect, 'openness' requires that such investment be sought through direct private foreign investment (DPI), since the reduction of the role of the state in the economy necessarily means that state investment is construed to be a form of interventionism and potential subsidy – which runs counter to subsidy reduction and privatization policies. Official Development Assistance (ODA) is also discouraged, except as a temporary substitute for private investment and DPI is seen as the appropriate alternative to it. Domestic private investment, of course, has to attend on economic development before it can play a significant role within the process of economic development.

The problem is that virtually all DPI worldwide comes from multinational corporations, which tend to be risk-adverse in their investment decisions. Peripheral economies undergoing economic restructuring with the attendant dangers of social and political unrest are not, therefore, attractive investment prospects. Furthermore, fully 80 per cent of all DPI annually goes to the "Triad" states of the EC, the USA and Japan and that proportion is rising. The developing world has seen its proportion of DPI fall from 18 per cent in the mid-1980s to around 15 per cent today. In addition, even though this might imply an absolute growth in value, much of the investment is insecure, since liberalized fiscal regimes allow for the easy repatriation of profits.

All-in-all, the developing world's attempt to attract DPI is failing, albeit with a few notable exceptions. The major success story, of course, has been Latin America, where Brazil and Mexico are seeing significant rises in DPI – mainly from funds being repatriated by nationals from abroad, and in some parts of Eastern Europe, such as Czechoslovakia and Hungary, where European multinational corporations have begun to invest and even here there are predictions of impending economic failure and crisis.[38] However, for the rest, the picture looks bleak. Even though the World Bank has recently suggested that DPI in the periphery will increase during the next decade, it admits that this will only occur in countries where there are well-developed infrastructures – a condition that does not apply for most of the developing world[39].

Conditionality

The outlook for economic development in the periphery thus looks generally bleak and is the result of a core-directed ideological intervention in the affairs of peripheral states in the developing world. Of course, there is no reason why investors – whether states or private entities – in the developed world should engage in economic intervention on conditions which they believe will fail. Equally, however, it is hardly reasonable for them to insist on conditions which are untried, the result of ideological prejudice and often require political conditions that run counter to the aspirations of the peoples concerned.

Conditionality is, however, the latest form of ideological interventionism that is designed to counter the development of adverse political structures. Conditionality requires that political reform must be undertaken over issues of observance of human rights and democratic practices as a counterpart to the provision of developmental aid of any kind. It is not yet a condition of IMF aid, nor, indeed, for aid from the World Bank. It is, however, required by individual states within the developed world, particularly those within the G-7 Group, and by the European Community. Yet conditionality flies in the face of the fact that economic reform of the type described above usually requires political authoritarianism for success and that private investment flows nearly always depend on political stability, not on political liberalization. 'Conditionality', therefore, seems to run counter to the whole neo-classical economic reform enterprise.

It is open to more serious objections than that, however. It is, first of all, a direct infringement in the sovereignty of the states concerned. Secondly, it takes no account of the specificity of the ideological change it requires. The concepts of human rights and democracy it imposes do not necessarily relate to the basic values of the societies on which they are imposed. Thirdly, the imposition ignores the fact that there is often no social or political consensus over the structure of the state involved, which is essential if democratic institutions are to survive[40], as the recent example of the failure of the democratic process in Algeria makes clear.

The issue is not whether or not populations seek legitimized government – so-called "good governance" – respect for human rights or recognition of minority rights. There is no doubt that they do. However, they seek authentic and culturally authenticated versions of these basic concepts. In the Middle East, at least, they do not believe the versions purveyed by the West, even by the United Nations, reflect these basic concerns. They therefore profoundly resent having such values imposed upon them, even if their governments cannot resist. The result is that government in the Middle East and North Africa is de-legitimized by the very process which is supposed to render it more legitimate. That, perhaps, is the most undesirable consequence of ideological intervention.

Finally, it does not allow for the lack of, nor encourage the growth of civil society in an essentially Hobbesian world. It is, in short a crass, insensitive and misguided attempt to impose an ideological straitjacket on the developing world which merely antagonizes and frustrates those on whom it is imposed. Yet, in a world which is not based on consensual discourse but on a hierarchy of power, there is little states in the periphery can do to counter such initiatives.

Conclusion

There is little support within the developing world, either in terms of international legal principle or in terms of global economic development or, even, in terms of popular support or theoretical approaches to international affairs, for the idea that certain states may abrogate to themselves rights of intervention – whether military or economic – in the affairs of other states, whatever the moral or legal justification for such acts, if, indeed, there is one. Rejection of such rights of intervention applies, in the eyes of states in the periphery, just as much to states within their world as it does to states from the developed world itself. It is, however, the case, that in recent years the most striking examples of such intervention have been initiated by states in the developed world so that the issue has increasingly come to be seen as an example of the North/ South divide within the context of the post-Cold War world. Equally, insofar as states within the periphery accept the implications of an international regime based on the United Nations, they also accept the diminuition in the absolute quality of state sovereignty that they claim. However, they cannot accept such a derogation of sovereign immunity when they perceive the United Nations – rightly or wrongly – to have become a vehicle of the ideological and policy preferences of leading states in the developed world. Once again, this appears to them to have been one of the consequences of the end of the Cold War.

It is in this context that the traditional view of the absolute quality of state sovereignty has become a touchstone of official opinion of states in the developing world. The concept of state sovereignty, together with the inherent rejection of the use of force in interstate relations as laid down in Article 2(4) of the United Nations Charter, should still, in the minds of their governments, at least, remain the fundamental guiding principle of international relations, together with the asso- ciated principle of the equality of all states within the world system. Within this framework of international obligation, intervention could only occur with the agreement, explicit or implicit, of the state concerned. There is, in short, no other general basis on which states may be sustained – quite apart from the interpretations of the implications of the end of the Cold War now widely accepted within the developing world – except through recognition of the basic integrity of the concept of state sovereignty:–

"Consider the dominance of the state system itself, the notion that political life must be territorially organized with one final authority within a given territory. Even if this vision is sometimes challenged, no alternative has been effectively articulated and legitimated ... But the triumph of sovereignty over other possible forms of political organization in the recent past is even more striking.

91

Efforts to convert colonial empires into commonwealths have failed. The Soviet effort to base relations in Eastern Europe on transnational functional agencies rather than on state-to-state agreements has eroded over time ... decolonization has led to the creation of a large number of states with only the most limited resources and populations. The existence of these states can hardly be explained by their material capabilities. Their survival and being are a function of the larger institutional framework in which they are embodied. Their most potent asset is not their tax base, population or army, but rather the juridical sovereignty that is accorded by the international community; that is, by the willingness of other states to endorse their existence and the absence of any alternative legitimate form for organizing political life."[41]

Yet, for these principles to be preserved, there must be attitudinal change within the core states of the developed world and institutional change within the United Nations. Leaderships within the developed world will have to abandon their triumphalism in the wake of the second Gulf war and the Cold War and accept the inherent absolute quality of state sovereignty and the equality of states within the global interstate system. They will also have to abandon the ideological enterprise implicit in the concept of 'the end of history'. In institutional terms, the United Nations Security Council will have to face reform: first, to end the veto power of the five permanent members and, second, either to remove the right to permanent membership or to adjust the nature of that membership to reflect the true demographic global balance. Only in this way can the peripheral states of the developing world be persuaded that a genuine world community can be created, in which the secession of sovereignty to international bodies does not threaten their integrity or their existence. There is, sadly, little likelihood that this will occur.

Notes

1. Maechling Jr, C., "Washington's illegal invasion", *Foreign Policy*, 79 (Summer 1990); 127.

2. Tian Jin, "Complexities of Human Rights in today's world", *Beijing Review*, *33*, (May 28–June 3, 1990); 10–12.

3. (Buzan B., "New patterns of global security in the twenty-first century", *Foreign Affairs*, *67*, 3 (1991); 431–451). Buzan's terminology divides the world into a multipolar core or centre dominated by the USA and a periphery which loosely corresponds to the old terminology of the "Third World", the "South" or the "developing world". His model is refined by suggesting that, for different purposes, some states in the periphery may move into the core or, as occurred during the Gulf war against Iraq, some peripheral states may associate themselves with the core for specific purposes to degrees defined by a series of concentric rings of different levels of interaction.

4. Maechling, "Washington's illegal intervention".; 113–16.

5. Roberts A., "A new age in international relations?", *International Affairs*, *67*, 3 (July 1991); 524–525.

6. see Østerud, p.21–22 for discussion of the Montevideo Convention.

7. ICJ Reports, 1949; 4,35.

8. see Chopra, p. 42–44 for discussion of the implications of the Corfu Channel case.

9. Akehurst, *A modern introduction to International law*; 112.

10. *viz* Chopra J. and Weiss T.G., "Sovereignty is no longer sacrosanct: codifying humanitarian intervention", *Ethics and International Affairs*, *6*, (1992); 95–117.

11. Chopra J. and Weiss T.C., "Sovereignty is no longer sacrosanct . . .";
102–03.

12. Wallace, *International Law*; 218.

13. Wallace, *International Law*; 104–106.

14. Wallace, *International Law*; 223–233.

15. Freysinger R.C. (1991), "US military and economic intervention in an international context of low-intensity conflict", *Political Studies*, *XXXIX*, June 1991; 333.

16. Webb M.C. and Krasner S.D., "Hegemonic stability theory: an empirical assessment", *Review of International Studies*, *15*, 2 (April 1989); 189.

17. *viz.* Cox R.W., "Multilateralism and world order", *Review of International Studies*, *18*, 2 (April 1992); 161–180.

18. See Byer B. (1991), "Ecoregions, state sovereignty and conflict", *Bulletin of Peace Proposals*, *22*, 1; 65–76.

19. Reisman M.W., "Sovereignty and human rights in contemporary international law", *The American Journal of International Law*, *84* (1990); 871.

20. *cf.* James A. (1992), "The equality of states: contemporary manifestations of an ancient doctrine", *Review of International Studies*, *18*, 4 (October 1992); 380–381.21.

Weber C. (1992), "Reconsidering statehood: examining the sovereignty/ intervention boundary", *Review of International Studies*, *18*, 3 (July 1992); 216.

22. Joffe E.G.H., "International law, conflict and stability in the Gulf and the Mediterranean", in Thomas C. and Saravanamuttu P. (eds), *The state and instability in the South*, London, Macmillan (1989); 167–171.

23. Maechling, "Washington's illegal invasion"; 122

24. Maechling, "Washington's illegal invasion"; 122–24.

25. D'Amato A., "The invasion of Panama was a lawful response to tyranny", *The American Journal of International Law*, *84* (April 1990); 516–524). His arguments were countered by Professor Ved P. Nanda, "US forces in Panama; defenders, aggressors or human rights activists?", and Professor T.J. Farer, "Panama: beyond the Charter paradigm", both in the same volume of *The American Journal of International Law*.

26. Chemillier-Gendreau M., "Politics and international law", *Contemporary European Affairs*, *4*, 1 (1991); 67–68.

27. Roberts, "A new age in international relations?"; 522.

28. See Pugh M., "Maritime operations; a break-out from peacekeeping?", unpublished paper, Southampton Project on UN Naval Peacekeeping Forces, February 14, 1992; 4.29.
    Mill J.S. (1867), "A few words on non-intervention", *Dissertations and discussions*, London, 1867; 168–69: cited by Mayall J., "Non-intervention, self determination and the 'new world order', *Foreign Affairs*, *67*, 3 (1991); 427.

30. Nardin T., "International ethics and international law", *Review of International Studies*, *18*, 1 (January 1992); 19–30.

31. Mayall, "Non-intervention, self-determination, and the 'new world order'"; 424: Thornberry P., "Self determination, minorities and human rights: a review of international instruments", *International and comparative law quarterly*, *38* (1989); 874–877.

32. Mayall, "Non-intervention, self-determination and the 'new world order'"; 424.

33. Heraclides, "Secessionist minorities and external involvement"; 351.

34. Mapel D.R., "Military intervention and rights"; 41–44.

35. The arguments presented here are drawn essentially from Niblock T. and Murphy E., *Economic and political liberalization in the Middle East*, Routledge London, British Academic Press, 1993, from Penrose E. (1992), "From economic liberalization to international integration: the role of the state", *ODA Review* (September 1992); Stevens P. (1989), "Privatization in the Middle East and North Africa", *Arab Affairs*, *10* (Autumn 1989); Penrose E., Joffe E.G.H. & Stevens P. (1992), "Nationalization of foreign-owned property for a public purpose: an economic perspective on appropriate compensation", *Modern Law*

Review (May 1992), Joffe E.G.H. (1990), "Privatization and decentralization in the Arab world, with special reference to Morocco", *JIME Review, 8* (Winter 1990) and Joffe E.G.H., "Foreign investment and economic liberalization", *JIME Review, 17* (Summer 1992).
36. Todaro M.P., *Economic development in the Third World*, 4th Edition, London, Longman, 1989; 83.
37. The World Bank, *World Development Report 1991: the challenge of development*, Oxford, Oxford University Press, 1991; 88.
38. Killick T. & Stevens C. (1991), "Eastern Europe:'lessons on economic adjustment from the Third World", *International Affairs, 67*, 4 (October 1991); 679–696.
39. World Bank, *World development Report*; 96.
40. For an illuminating account of the degree of hostility initiatives such as 'conditionality' can arouse, see Dwyer K., *Arab Voices: the human rights debate in the Middle East*; London, Routledge, 1991.
41. Krasner S.D., "Sovereignty, an institutional perspective", *Comparative Political Studies, 21*, 1 (April 1988); 66–94.

Chapter 4

The United Nations and Intra-State Conflicts

Åge Eknes

The United Nation's system for collective security was conceived in a fundamentally different political context from that it has had to adapt to. The Cold War made the Charter provisions for coercive action obsolete. By and large the UN became an inept intermediary called upon, albeit rarely, by contending parties when they needed practical assistance in order to contain or settle a conflict. But whereas the ongoing changes in international politics have increased the UN's status and ability to use coercive means, the same changes have also facilitated a shift in the nature of the conflicts on the organization's agenda which again have challenged other basic assumptions of the UN Charter.

One of the most controversial issues in this respect, is UN involvement, in particular military involvement, in conflicts taking place within the boundaries of member states: Intra-state conflicts are growing dramatically both in number and in importance as the repression mechanisms of the Cold War have vanished and national sovereignty erodes as a consequence of challenges from within as well as above the state.[1]

From Principles to Pragmatism

The UN Charter places the "primary responsibility for the maintenance of international peace and security"[2] upon the Security Council. But the UN's rights and responsibilities when it comes to handling internal conflicts are more ambiguous. It has always been emphasized that a fundamental objective for the organization is to protect the territorial integrity and political independence of its members, a principle the UN so far has, with very few exceptions, been careful to observe. In the Cold War period, it became a political axiom that the UN Charter represented an almost absolute hinder against involvement by the organization in such affairs, despite the much more nuanced legal debate that took place simultaneously. The principle of non-intervention was claimed by the UN as well as state leaders in order to legitimize inaction when Pol Pot and Idi Amin committed their genocides in Cambodia and Uganda, civil war raged in East Pakistan and Saddam Hussein used chemical weapons against his Kurdish population in the late 1980s.

Not so any more. The UN is becoming increasingly more involved in attempts to contain or alleviate what traditionally has been perceived as internal conflicts, primarily in its peacekeeping capacity, but also with coercive measures. The change has occurred rapidly. In the spring of 1991, Security Council (SC) resolution 688, which provided the basis for the US led coalition that intervened in northern Iraq to protect the Kurds, was heavily criticized because it was seen by many as an unacceptable intervention in a country's domestic affairs. As the war escalated in the former Yugoslavia barely a year later, similar objections against a more comprehensive and forceful UN role were more or less non-existent. The controversy this time became how to intervene – partly because there existed diverging interpretations internationally concerning the causes of the conflict and partly because no one was able to prescribe instruments for more forceful intervention that were perceived as likely to terminate the conflict at an acceptable cost. However, in Somalia where the political as well as military situation was more clear cut, a US led intervention took place in December 1992 with, initially, almost universal support.

But the shift towards a more interventionist approach can also be observed in the official records of the UN. For example, whereas, the Secretary General's report of June 1992 on measures to strengthen the UN, "An Agenda for Peace", initially emphasized the importance of state sovereignty as the foundation stone of the international order, many of his concrete proposals were aimed at strengthening the organizations ability to assist in terminating internal conflicts.

Suddenly, intervening or not has become as much a practical question as a legal one. Contemporary tragedies in former Yugoslavia and Somalia have triggered a debate regarding when and how it is morally right and practically realistic to intervene. International public opinion demands action and moves often reluctant governments to address issues which they until recently could repudiate on a formal basis. New thinking is taking place with regard to how intervention, in particular military intervention, might be performed. "Costs", "dangers" and "chances of success" are suddenly more often discussed than international law when world leaders consider if and how they can unravel situations like Sarajevo.

One of the interesting characteristics of the present debate is the new emphasis on collective intervention, or more precisely, intervention by international organizations like the UN. Whereas, the zero-sum game of the Cold War was used to justify unilateral intervention in just about any conflict, there has emerged a new demand for legitimization. It is becoming a rare event to see countries muddling into the affairs of others in an extensive manner without some kind of UN authorization, claimed or real. Equally interesting, countries hampered by civil wars now turn to the UN to obtain third party assistance in order to find a practical way to establish peace. In fact, a clear majority of the UN peacekeeping operations established since the end of the Cold War have been deployed in intra-state situations or conflicts with a clear internal dimension. "International peace and security" has a broader meaning than before. And not without reason. As the tragedy in former Yugoslavia illustrates, what in the summer of 1991 commenced as a civil war became in less than a year an international war involving four states which have emerged from the same territory and the violence threatens to engulf neighbouring countries.

The UN and Domestic Jurisdiction

Broad references to the "UN Charter" were often used during the Cold War in order to argue that the UN had no role in internal conflicts unless it was invited in by the parties, if even then. However, the argument was at best oversimplified and definitely more of a political than legal character.

Article 2(7) of the UN Charter restricts the organization's right to interfere in the domestic politics of the member states. This article has been described as a rather clumsy attempt to reconcile the doctrine of state sovereignty with the need to open for intervention when a domestic situation deteriorates or becomes a international concern.[3] The article provides that:

"Nothing contained in the present charter shall authorize the United Nations to intervene in matters which are essentially within the domestic jurisdiction of any State or shall require the members to submit such matters to settlement under the present Charter; but this principle shall not prejudice the application of enforcement measures under Chapter VII."

The meaning of Article 2 (7) is unclear. A narrow interpretation prevents the Security Council from any involvement in internal conflicts, or on issues within the domestic jurisdiction of states, unless it first decides that the situation represents a threat or breach of the peace according to Article 39 and successively takes action according to Article 41 or 42. But this interpretation is stricter than what the majority of the founding fathers had in mind. The drafters' problem was to find a way to express that "it would be proper in the interests of peace and justice, and in the preservation of human rights to interfere in the internal affairs of Member States".[4]

From the early writings on Article 2(7) it has been emphasized that the concept of domestic jurisdiction is relative.[5] No state has ever been free and independent to do as it pleased as the UN's founding fathers were well aware. The understanding of sovereignty changes with time and space. Pollution was, if an issue at all, a domestic concern some decades back. Now it has gained a position on the UN's as well as other international organizations agendas. Similarly, democratic values and human rights are matters of considerable international concern for Western democracies, but many Third World regimes tend to place a different emphasis on their importance. The question then becomes who decides? Who has the superior right to define whether a conflict which takes place within the boundaries of a state is within the domestic jurisdiction or not: the individual members or the UN? Despite a long history of claims to the opposite, the political organs of the UN established at an early stage a practice whereby they decided by themselves about their own competence by placing or not placing an issue on the agenda.

The UN Charter is not without contradictions. A long legal debate has also taken place with regard to the status of article 2(7) vis-a-vis other provisions of the UN Charter, in particular those which guarantee human and minority rights (articles 1, 13, 55, 56). Proponents of non-intervention argue that Article 2(7) is an overriding provision, that "Nothing contained in the present Charter" means nothing regardless of possible violations of other parts of the Charter. Although conflicts between these principles tended to be decided in favour of non-intervention during the Cold War, it is a generally accepted principle of treaty interpretation that:

"No part of a treaty should be interpreted in isolation and independently of the rest of its provisions. Article 2(7) cannot, therefore, have an absolute meaning and effect in itself; its meaning is relative to the other provisions of the Charter."[6]

And further:

"... a cardinal principle of treaty interpretation is that the parties must not be presumed to have intended to nullify or stultify a treaty by defeating its very purposes; and there is every reason to believe this rule of treaty interpretation applicable to the Charter, for its drafters could hardly have intended to render virtually inapplicable the clauses on the general purposes of the United Nations, its powers of

discussion, and its projected work for human rights . . .".[7]
As it sporadically became involved in internal conflicts, the Security Council gradually developed its own interpretation of the constraints Article 2(7) places upon its activity. The debate following the UN force in Congo in the early 1960s ended with the understanding that action taken under Chapter VII, whether enforcement or not, is not limited by Article 2(7). The argument behind this is that Chapter VII action inevitably means that international peace and security is threatened or violated. This makes the exception in the article (use of enforcement measures) redundant since the conflict is, thus, lifted above the domestic context. This implies, among other things, that the Council in such situations can utilize whatever measures it has at its disposal in dealing with international security.

Similarly, the doctrine on situations of "international concern", which was developed in the early years of the UN, further circumvented a strict interpretation of Article 2 (7). This argues that a finding of a potential threat to the peace represents a sufficient basis for the Council to become involved in a domestic conflict and, moreover, that the Council in such situations can act under Chapter VI as well as VII. ". . . the Council can utilize the provisions of Chapter VI and the power to ask for voluntary measures in the face of the provisions of Article 2(7)".[8]

There is a need to examine what intervention means in a UN context.[9] At least it is important to distinguish it from some of the more dubious and aggressive unilateral activities often associated with the concept. Intervention, a word generally avoided within the UN, is often understood as something unacceptable and illegal. Most often intervention is executed by individual states or even groups of states with specific interests in the country concerned. The word is, therefore, normally used by the critics of a specific action. The interventionists will inevitably explain or defend the action in other terms. But there exist several legal as well as political aspects which make UN intervention quite different from unilateral intervention. Three aspects seem to be of particular importance.

First, UN intervention is by definition intervention which has

been authorized by an international body with widespread legitimacy. In most cases, the country targeted will be a member which has violated the UN Charter in ways the political organs of the organization deem unacceptable. UN intervention is, therefore, intervention with a higher degree of *legitimacy* than unilateral intervention.

Second, UN intervention differs in *objective* from unilateral intervention committed by individual states in order to promote their own national interests regardless of the rhetoric used to defend it. If the UN intervenes, it is by definition in order to defend or restore the principles upon which it is built and to which the country concerned has committed itself by its membership. It might be argued, as it has been on some recent occasions, that UN intervention often is nothing but a guise for unilateral intervention by a powerful state, or groups of states, which is capable of dominating the UN's decision-making bodies. This argument bears some merit. However, there exists no institutional framework which contains better safety mechanisms against such misuse.

Finally, UN intervention differs in *methods* from unilateral intervention. Whilst unilateral intervention might take a number of rather subversive and illegal forms, the UN is restricted to methods envisaged in its Charter. Such intervention will have a completely different degree of transparency. This implies that the organization will have to justify the means used and the objectives sought in a manner completely different from unilateral interveners acting on self-interest.

What then constitutes UN intervention? The concept is difficult to define. It is always a question of more or less. The word has been used to describe everything from the inclusion of a topic on the Agenda of the General Assembly, through fact-finding, the passing of resolutions, peacekeeping, implementation of sanctions to forceful military intervention. However, to label the entire spectrum, "intervention", would make the concept hollow and difficult to use. The UN, therefore, decided at an early stage that the establishment of commissions or deployment of observers in order to establish facts in a domestic conflict did not constitute intervention. But the involved parties might be of a different opinion even at such a minimum level of UN involvement. The negative connotations of intervention, and the difficulties in distinguishing it from less coercive activities, might argue for the use of words like "involvement" instead of "intervention" when UN activities of this kind are addressed.

Likewise, there is a need to distinguish between the various political bodies of the UN. Both the General Assembly and the Secretary General have acted, and will probably continue to do so, in manners which individual states or governments have resented. However, it is only the Council that has the authority to make mandatory decisions and authorize enforcement measures in order to have them implemented. In most situations, therefore, there is a substantial difference between UN actions which involve the Council and those which do not.

The Cold War experience

US-Soviet power struggle deprived the UN of its intended role. Its involvement became restricted to situations where the parties, or rather the governments involved, consented to a UN role, or in rare exceptions, when the veto powers of the Council reached agreement on mandatory action in relation to conflicts outside their direct zones of influence. The UN's role in internal conflicts was, if possible, even more restricted than in inter-state turmoil.

But despite this, during the first four decades of its existence, the UN did involve itself in civil wars on a number of occasions and in a variety of ways. It acted under chapter VI as well as VII. It passed resolutions, established fact-finding missions, deployed observers and peacekeepers, implemented economic sanctions and authorized use of military force in situations of domestic unrest. The Security Council, as well as the General Assembly and the Secretary General, were involved. Hence, it is not absence of involvement in intra-state conflict which is the most characteristic feature of this period, but the low level of involvement and the lack of consistent behaviour when, or if, the UN and, in particular, the Council eventually managed to act. The widespread tendency of unilateral, and at times somewhat questionable unilateral intervention, by the prominent members of the Council in most conflict areas made the UN's insignificance all the more obvious.

For example, as early as in 1946, the Council became involved in an internal conflict when it established a Commission of Investigation in order to report on aspects of the Greek Civil War. At the same time it also set up a sub-committee to investigate the activities of the Franco regime and assess whether it endangered international peace and security. Although Soviet opposition prevented further UN action, these two examples highlight that an investigation to ascertain the facts, and even to make substantive recommendations in civil war situations, is not considered to be outside the competence of the Council.[10] However, Cold War history provides many more examples of unsuccessful efforts to establish such missions and of the UN's inability to act upon its findings. Nonetheless, recent moves to send UN fact finders to Central America, South Africa and Nagorno Karabach have their Cold War precedence.

Similarly, even if the UN's concept of peacekeeping was primarily developed in order to deal with interstate conflicts, this technique, although often in a modified form, was early on introduced in situations of internal turbulence. UN forces were sent to Congo as well as to Cyprus in the early 1960s in order to pacify civil conflicts. In the first case, the UN soldiers were sent in order to assist the government with ensuring law and order. In the latter, the mission's primary task was to interposition itself between warring Greek and Turk communities. Other Cold War peacekeeping missions, for example UNIFIL in Lebanon, were established to control an international conflict with obvious internal dimensions.

During the Cold War period, UN intervention, with enforcement measures against a regime in order to impose a specific internal political change, was confined to the fight against Apartheid. The first example was the economic sanctions imposed against former Rhodesia. In 1966 the Council also authorized the United Kingdom to establish a naval blockade of the Mozambiqan harbour of Beira in order to prevent oil from reaching the country, a blockade that was upheld by the British Navy until 1975. The UN never adopted equally decisive measures in its campaign against South Africa. Whereas the General Assembly repeatedly called for mandatory economic sanctions, the Council could not reach agreement on more than an arms embargo and voluntary severance of cultural and sports relations.

Another sombre characteristic of this period was the UN's and, particularly, the Council's inability to implement its own decisions when, or if, it managed to act. The countries embroiled in conflict as well as other UN members took the resolutions only as seriously as befitted their interests. The Council's ability to follow up with stronger measures, if resolutions were ignored, were literally non-existent. Indeed, the permanent members of the Council were often among the most prominent violators. With regard to peacekeeping operations, missions in intra-state turmoil were hampered as much as those deployed in inter-state conflicts by the Council's negligence or lack of political and economic support.

Current Trends

Much has been turned upside down within the UN over the past five years. The traditional and rather ineffective block voting system in the Security Council has disappeared and has been replaced by tighter cooperation among the five permanent members on most issues. For all practical purposes, they now decide both which issues shall be allowed on the Council's agenda as well as on decisions taken. If the five reach agreement, a majority of the Council's members will inevitably follow. Further, the permanent members have literally given up the use of their veto. The veto members now tend to abstain when they are reluctant to accept a Council initiative, thereby, allowing the UN to act despite their hesitation. On those rare occasions that permanent members have signalled their intension to block a specific proposal that has been discussed, this has either been modified or withdrawn by the sponsors in order to avoid a formal veto. As Brian Urquhart, among others, has pointed out, the UN has never been closer to the collective security ideals of 1945 than today.[11]

This has meant that the UN's overall involvement in peace

and security issues has increased notably. The trend has been reinforced by the fact that even major powers do not possess the necessary economic resources in order to act as global policemen, nor do they possess the moral weight to do so.[12] Conflicts which traditionally were kept alive by Cold War rivalry, such as the civil war in Angola, have suddenly emerged on the UN's agenda. Others, which have become violent as a result of the vanishing repression of the Cold War, have also ended on the UN's table.[13] Further, the Council's new willingness to use the entire spectre of available measures in dealing with security issues have elevated the UN's credibility beyond its shaky Cold War reputation. The major powers have on several occasions pressed for authorization of coercive measures in order to ensure that the Council's decisions are observed in a more effective manner than hitherto. But as the sanctions against Belgrade and Baghdad illustrate: one thing is to act with force, another to achieve the desired results.

The increased volume of UN activity, and in particular the increased number of Blue Helmets, have created an institutional challenge for the UN. The gap between the tasks given and the available means for handling them is distressing. To take one example: The staff in the UN secretariat responsible for peacekeeping was insufficient for its Cold War tasks. Today the UN has deployed more soldiers than the authorized strength of all UN peacekeeping missions until 1988. In fact, the number increased from about 10 000 in early 1992 to above 50 000 a year later. The UN has now more soldiers in active service than many mid-sized nations and the number continues to increase. They are deployed all over the globe, with highly varying tasks and often in unstable operational environments. But a noticeable strengthening of the UN's military staff has not taken place, in fact it is still smaller than that of, for example, a brigade in a NATO country. This has made it difficult for the UN to move beyond the Cold War practice of responding in ad hoc manners to specific cases or situations since it has failed to address itself adequately to the more overall principles and problems of the UN's new and expanded military role. The summit meeting of the Council in January 1992 and the Secretary General's "Agenda for Peace" represent efforts to move beyond this, so far without concrete results.

However, some changes are in progress. The UN has encouraged the ongoing development of regional security arrangements. According to Chapter VIII of the Charter, such arrangements might be utilized in order to resolve local conflicts and, thereby, relieve some of the present pressure. In Europe, for example, the CSCE, EC and NATO have all been involved in conflicts in former Yugoslavia and to a more limited degree in the former Soviet Union. But as the Yugoslav tragedy proved, especially in the early phase, unless the efforts of the UN and the regional organizations become better coordinated, the number of cooks might make it difficult to agree upon a workable recipe despite the considerable amount of available resources. Besides, increased reliance on regional organizations by the Western states might be perceived by developing countries as attempt to escape responsibility. Many regions in the Third World do not possess adequate resources for developing strong regional security structures.

The most noticeable feature of the post Cold War security agenda of the Council is the shift away from traditional inter-state conflicts, to conflicts which stem from ethnic animosities within states or government denial of minority and human rights. In fact, despite the Iraqi invasion of Kuwait and the Arab-Israeli conflict, such conflicts have for the past four years dominated the UN's agenda and they are likely to continue to do so. Nearly two-thirds of the UN's peacekeeping missions established after 1988 have dealt with intra-state problems and the major bulk of UN mediation has taken place in internal or ethnic conflicts in Central America, Africa, Europe and Asia.

Although to a large degree this trend is a consequence of the disappearance of the Cold War, other and perhaps less appreciated factors are involved:

The first is the waning authority of the UN's constituent unit; the state. Non-state actors, such as Amnesty International and the Red Cross, have for years practised a rather "flexible" interpretation of sovereignty when this has been necessary to assist people who have become victims of government atrocities.[14] Their right to do so has rarely been challenged by others than the government involved. To the contrary, such action has in many situations received massive international support as well as reinforced criticism of states for their lack of decisive action.

Second, with the relative authority of sovereign states diminishing, nationalism and new sub-national actors have gained momentum. Many state structures are today not capable of handling the present upsurge in ethnic violence and the secessionist demands which often follows.

Third, the combination of increased international concern for human rights and the ability of international media to focus on suffering irrespective of boundaries, have made the individual's world smaller and his awareness of others higher. A massive campaign by the international media is impossible for politicians to ignore regardless whether the television lens is focused on Rumanian orphanages or the shelling of Sarajevo.

Fourth, the emphasis international opinion has placed on potential global disasters has changed the way people think about security. Environmental threats and the consequences of the unequal and unjust distribution of the world's resources are now issues which are gaining security status both in people's minds and in the UN. The same holds for the increased availability of weapons of mass destruction and the technology to develop them as the Council already have demonstrated by its demands for the destruction of Iraq's capacity to build and deliver such weapons.

Fifth, subversive activity of criminal non-state actors, such as mafias, terrorists and drug traffickers, is posed to enter the international security agenda in a more comprehensive manner than hitherto. This does not mean that these issues will be confined exclusively to the UN's agenda. The Secretary General's successful involvement in negotiating the release of Western hostages held captive by different militias in Lebanon illustrates one important role the UN can have in this respect.

Institutional Weaknesses

The UN's response to these challenges has so far mainly been of an ad hoc character and not without contradictions and obvious weaknesses. Some factors are rather self-evident, others more controversial and obscure.

One of the most obvious weaknesses is the gap between willingness and ability to act. The UN has never acquired the military enforcement capacity envisaged in the Charter. Its Blue Helmets were designed to function more as negotiators than as enforcers. Their weapons have primarily been for self defense. But as UN involvement in Lebanon, Yugoslavia and Somalia have demonstrated, achieving the same degree of cooperation and consent among the numerous and vaguely defined parties in a civil war as in traditional inter-state conflicts simply cannot be expected. The result is that the UN now deploys soldiers in formations and with mandates which obviously are insufficient for anything but "best case scenarios". Peacekeeping missions, composed of soldiers from numerous different countries with different languages and military training, do not possess the necessary qualifications for rapid and consistent military action which such situations demand. [15]Episodes such as those during the initial phase of the operation in Somalia, when US soldiers had to secure the arrival of UN soldiers, do not contribute to strengthening the UN's military credibility. Until the UN achieves some degree of convincing military capacity on a level between current Blue Helmets operations and that of regular military formations, as called for by "Agenda for Peace", the UN's ability to respond to humanitarian catastrophes and civil wars will be limited, often hazardous and always characterized by ad hoc solutions.

Second, these new missions have also highlighted the lack of clarity concerning the competence between the different UN bodies and between the UN and other security organizations which might reduce its impact on the conflict. Yugoslavia is a case in point. Here the Secretary General first cautioned, in vain, the EC against recognizing the secessionist republics. Subsequently, a controversy between him and the Council ensued concerning the size and budget of the UN force in Croatia (UNPROFOR). As the civil war in Bosnia Hercegovina came to a peak, the relationship between the Secretary General and the EC became tense as the latter tried to instruct the UN to perform tasks the Secretary General claimed it had neither capacity nor authority to perform. Thereafter,

European countries, led by the two West European permanent members of the Council, planned, deployed and financed the expansion of UNPROFOR with a so-called Bosnia-Hercegovina Command almost without communication and coordination with the UN Secretariat that led the initial force in Croatia.

Finally, the UN's increased involvement in internal unrest has triggered a new demand for consistency. The Secretary General stated in the spring of 1992 that the Council's lack of willingness to act on the basis of the same principles when Somalia was on the agenda as when former Yugoslavia was debated, undermined the UN's credibility in the Third World. A year later, critics reversed the argument as the UN involvement in Somalia increased and the Council failed to reach agreement on use of similar means in Bosnia.

The US and its Western allies' insistence on using UN resolutions as a legitimating basis for its repeated interference in Iraq might also backfire on the UN. Lack of an undisputable overall UN control gives nurture to allegations regarding a Western or major power dominated UN which acts highly selectively and abuses the organization to serve narrow national interests. As Brian Urquhart has pointed out, "The truth of the matter is that intervention at the moment is ruled by the power of the purse and the power of the veto. This is an extremely divisive situation."[16]

Future Challenges

The UN's imminent challenge is, of course, to close the gap between its willingness and ability to act in international as well as internal conflicts. "An Agenda for Peace" proposes a number of steps, some of which has been discussed for years without receiving the necessary support. Among the issues considered are:

1. Increasing the UN's ability to prevent or act at an early stage by establishing a better system for early warning and preventive diplomacy.
2. Improving the peacekeeping machinery by establishing a system whereby governments earmark military units for

such purposes. Financing of such missions should be secured by the establishment of a special fund, and an adequate standard of the units secured by establishing training programmes.

3. Establishment of "peace enforcement units", that is specially trained and equipped units which can be deployed under unstable operational environments, for example, to impose a violated cease-fire.

4. Establishment of the UN Charter provisions for collective security according to Article 42 and 43, i.e. earmarking forces for use by the Security Council.

These proposals have now been debated in different UN bodies for more than a year without leading to substantial decisions. However, even if improvements within any of these areas will increase its capacity to intervene, a certain reservation should also be expressed. In the long run it would be dangerous and counterproductive for the UN to develop a might to intervene in domestic situations without clarifying its right to do so in more detail than hitherto. It is of fundamental importance to develop legal norms for intervention, norms or principles which would be more evenhandedly applied than what we today witness.[17] There must be an answer to why it was so much easier for the Western permanent members of the Council to use military power in Iraq and Somalia than in Bosnia-Hercegovina.

This problem is also closely linked to an inevitable discussion on the composition of the UN and in particular the Security Council. Today this reflects the political realities of the middle of this century rather than the end of it. With the dissolution of the Soviet Union, the three Western members are now *de facto* in a position where they can force through almost any resolution they might want. We could, thus, experience a rapid marginalization of the UN's security role if these countries repeatedly use the Council to give themselves "collective legitimation" for intervention in situations where they have only limited international support. It is difficult to imagine any long term solution which does not in one way or another alter the membership of the Council substantially in order to make it more representative.

111

But the question of composition has also another important aspect. The UN is a collection of states in a period of waning state sovereignty and, in many case, legitimacy. This seems to be an irreversible trend which could mean that the UN will become less able to cope with tomorrow's security agenda since many new actors are left out. The arguments that exist to support demands for enlarging the UN membership with representation from, for instance, national minorities are highly relevant. Why should not Kosovo's approximately 2 million Albanians have a seat in the UN when Iceland's population of 250,000 have one? However, with roughly some 1700 national minorities in the world and over 100 within Russia alone an expansion along these lines would not strengthen the UN's ability to act decisively. And which criteria should be used to qualify minorities for UN representation?

Finally, the UN's right to involve itself in internal conflicts must be assessed in the light of what it is able to achieve. Much of the debate today focuses on the need to alleviate suffering and contain violence in contrast to create peace – implying that the former objectives are easier to achieve and, thus, should have priority. In some situations, this assessment might be correct. However, one could also argue that intervention in favour of the Kurds in 1991 and of the Shia Muslims of southern Iraq in 1992 have reduced the chances for finding a settlement between them and the regime in Baghdad. It is, therefore, relevant to query humanitarian intervention which might create even more long term humanitarian suffering. At least there exists a need to further refine this concept in order to reduce or minimize such effects. The Secretary General's "Agenda for Peace" emphasizes post-conflict peace-building. Whereas, in many situations an inter-state conflict can be contained by a limited number of peacekeepers with moderate costs for decades, internal situations tend to be more complex and unstable. Even a strengthened military presence will not necessarily contain the underlying tensions generating violence in a Kurdistan, a Bosnia or a Somalia. Military action by the UN to stop or manage conflict needs to be linked to political measures in order to create peace. The UN's major problem in this respect is that the tools at its disposal for conflict management were designed for use in traditional inter-state conflict in a political context that is now gone. This is an area that needs immediate attention. Otherwise, the organization risks becoming overwhelmed by a high number of interminable conflicts.

The UN has already started, characteristically by focusing on a specific case rather than on the principle. In Cambodia, the UN force, UNTAC, *de facto* took control of large parts of the state apparatus in the transition period.[18] Even if UNTAC did not achieve the desired results and displayed a number of internal weaknesses, it represented a major step towards developing a more comprehensive approach to civil war situations. This kind of comprehensive effort aimed at identifying and strengthening structures and processes necessary to establish peace might be of equal, if not, more importance in, for example, a settlement of the conflicts in Bosnia and Somalia. Thus UNTAC has contributed to a growing debate of the relevance of revitalizing and modifying the UN's system of Trusteeships, whereby, the UN takes control and responsibility for the administration of a country or territory in a transition period until the local political structures are capable of taking over. Even if neither the name or the original concept is directly applicable today, it is difficult to envisage alternatives. In fact, intellectuals in Sarajevo in the early stages of the conflict in Bosnia-Hercegovina called for a UN presence in the country based upon a flexible interpretation of Chapter XIII of the Charter.[19] The proposal was viewed as unrealistic both because of its price tag and the enormous political and military tasks involved. However, if UN soldiers were deployed throughout Bosnia at an early stage with a mandate to disarm the fractions and ensure the withdrawal of foreign forces, the war might have been prevented. And if UN representatives had been inserted in the political structures of the country in order to facilitate a conciliatory and democratic development, it might have been possible to establish a independent and democratic Bosnia-Hercegovina at lesser cost for the international society than it is potentially confronting.

Conclusion

The UN has received a second chance to become the leading organization for international peace and security in accordance with the expectations of 1945. But in order to grasp this opportunity, it needs not only to implement the provisions of the Charter that remained dormant during the Cold War, it must also adapt to the world and its troubles five decades later.

Among the most sensitive issues in this respect, will be the handling of conflicts which individual states might claim to be within their domestic jurisdiction when large parts of the international society hold the opposite view. This article has argued that the UN's right to intervene in such situations are both morally and legally far broader than usually acknowledged. In fact, the UN's overall purpose of maintaining international peace and security depends to a large extent upon its ability to control unrest with intra-state roots.

Whilst there exists a growing acceptance of the UN's right and obligation to involve itself in such situations, its practical ability to do so is at present highly limited. Today's system is open to misuse. The tools at the UN's disposal are at best insufficient. The immediate problems are of a practical kind. They involve developing military and political strategies which can be used in such situations without endangering UN lives to an unacceptable degree and which have the capacity for making a difference.

Notes

1. See Jarat Chopra in this volume and J. Chopra and T. G. Weiss, "Sovereignty is no Longer Sacrosanct: Codifying Humanitarian Intervention," *Ethics and International Affairs, vol 6, 1992, pp. 95–117.*
2. UN Charter Art. 24.1.
3. N. D. White "The United Nations and the Maintenance of International Peace and Security" Manchester University Press 1990.
4. Report of the Conference held in San Francisco by the Rt Hon. Peter Frazer, Chairman of the New Zealand delegation. Quoted from N D White 1990:50.
5. See R. Higgins: *The Development of International Law through the Organs of the United Nations,* Oxford University Press 1963.

6. Rajan (1961) quoted from Higgins (1963:65).
7. R Higgins op cit p.
8. N. D. White 1990:51.
9. See Stanley Hoffmann "The Problem of Intervention" and Evan Luard "Collective Intervention" in Hedley Bull (ed) *Intervention in World Politics*, Clarendon Press, Oxford 1984.
10. N.D. White op.cit. pg. 51.
11. Brian Urquhart "Learning from the Gulf" *The New York Review of Books* March 7. 1991 pp. 34–37.
12. Eduard Shevardnadze quoted in J. Mackinlay and J. Chopra "Second Generation Multinational Operations" *The Washington Quarterly,* Vol. 15 Issue 3, 1992.
13. For an overview of recent UN military operations, see for example W. J. Durch and B. M. Blechman "Keeping the Peace: The United Nations in the Emerging World Order" The Stimson Center March 1992.
14. See for example T. G. Weiss and Kurt Cambell "Military Humanitarianism", *Survival*, Vol.xxxiii, No.5, 1991, pp.451–465.
15. For example, both UNTAC in Cambodia and UNPROFOR in Croatia had 29 participating countries in May 1992 and the number of troop contributors are likely to increase.
16. Commentary by Brian Urquhart to Stanley Hoffmann's "Ethics of Humanitarian Intervention" in a report published by *The Harvard Center for Population and Development Studies*, Cambridge, 1991.
17. See Stanley Hoffmann "The Ethics of Humanitarian Intervention" op. cit.
18. See for example J. Chopra, John mackinlay and Larry Minear "Report on the Cambodian Peace Process" *NUPI Report No. 165, February 1993* The Norwegian Institute of International Affairs.
19. See Stojan Pajic, "UN Trusteeship Can Halt Ethnic Ghettoes", *YUGOFAX* nb. 11, London May 1992.

Chapter 5

Tribal and International Law, Between Right and Might

Ernest Gellner

The issue of sovereignty and intervention, dispute mediation by consent or by force have so far in this volume been considered mainly in relation to the international institutions and laws of contemporary society. Yet these concerns were also central to and arguably managed in a similar way by tribal institutions and customary law. To illustrate the point I shall take an example from Morocco.

Until a few decades ago, Morocco was tribally organized, and retains marked traces of that organization to this day. One aspect of that organization was the use of tribal customary law, preserved – or created – in the memory of elders, rather than in recorded legislation.

During the colonial period in Morocco, the existence of this tribal customary law became a major political issue. In the course of their slow conquest of traditionally "dissident" tribal areas, French authorities generally offered tribes, as an additional inducement for submission, the option of retaining their custom, as opposed to being subjected to the general legal code prevalent in the country as a whole. This practice was confirmed by a decree (dahir) formally signed by the then Sultan, but in fact inspired by the colonial power, in 1930. The promulgation of this decree triggered off a wave of protest not only within Morocco but in other Muslim lands, as far east as Indonesia. The logic of the protest was that such a confirmation or encouragement of tribal heterodoxy, distinct from Koranically orthodox central legislation, was an attempt at driving a wedge between Muslims, possibly even a first step in an attempt to convert the Berbers. The protest movement against this measure is generally treated by historians as the starting point of modern Moroccan nationalism.

This issue is not directly relevant to our present purpose. What is very highly relevant is one of the central and most characteristic practices deployed within this tribal legal system, namely trial by collective oath. It is an institution found in many tribal or loosely organized societies, Muslim and other. I shall describe a schematized version of this procedure, as it functioned amongst Berber tribes of the Atlas mountains. The baseline of any account must of course be the observation that litigants or plaintiffs, individuals or groups in conflict, do not and cannot in the very nature of this kind of society appear and operate *as* individuals, or as *isolated* groups. They simply must have their place in a wider system of groups, usually "nested" in a neat manner; they must have their location on a social map.

In the case of an individual, what is central for his social identity, is that he has such and such a set of (literal) brothers, defined by descent from the same father, and such and such a set of patrilineal cousins, defined by descent from the same paternal grandfather, and so forth. These nested sets of ever-larger groups, defined by real or fictive agnatic kinship (and sometimes, by ritual incorporation, or by territory), defines the basic legal and political organization of the tribal territory. Like citizenship in a territorial state, it defines a person's identity, but also (or thereby) articulates the social units which not only ascribe inheritance and other rights (including rights to brides), but also ensures a person's security. A person is legally responsible for his agnatic kin, and they are responsible for him. If a member of such a group commits an offence against the member of a rival group, and a *feud* ensues, *all* members of the group become potential victims of retaliation – not the culprit alone. If the conflict is terminated by the payment of appropriate compensation, the entire group contributes or receives the payment.

Now it is possible to describe the mechanism of a collective oath. Suppose a man is accused of an offence, be it a theft, a rape, or a murder. The alleged offence is normally committed against the member of *another* agnatic group, another nation if you will, who constitute the accusers. The issue can be settled by a solemn oath, taken by the male kin of the accused, in order of proximity to him (which is also the order in which they have claims on his estate in case of his decease). The oath is taken in a sacred place, sometimes a mosque, more often a shrine of a saint. The number of cojurors required will vary with the gravity of the offence: a theft of a sheep may only call for two oaths, the murder of a woman may require twenty, the murder of a man, forty. The accusation is held to be invalid if those required to perform the oath do so without stumbling, without failing to utter the prescribed formula, in brief if they are both willing and able to testify properly, and if whilst doing so they are not smitten with some dreadful punishment. The theory of the whole process is of course that the supernatural, and the fear of the supernatural, is enlisted so that justice should be done. Fear of the supernatural will inhibit the willingness to testify falsely, and punish, either at once by supernatural means, or perhaps later by natural ones, those who have borne false witness. (Though it should be noted that the cojurors are not necessarily in possession of the relevant information, though of course they are familiar with the character of the accused and hence with the plausibility of the accusation: they are guarantors, rather than witnesses in the Western sense.)

It is important to note the prima facie absurdity of this system. Legal cases are decided in effect by juries, which are selected in terms of social proximity to the accused! In other words, the decision is entrusted to those whose interests must strongly incline them to find him innocent. Moreover, this system operates in a society which places extremely great value on group cohesion and on solidarity between agnatic kinsmen. Similar to the modern international order of independent states, this system is markedly lacking in institutions which would underwrite a more abstract, symmetrical loyalty to abstract rules of rectitude which are blind to the links of blood. All this being so, would not such a system result, inevitably and mechanically, in universal acquittals? What else could it possibly lead to? And what possible use could there be in a system which so predictably, so insensitively, leads to but one possible result?

Unquestionably, the system was in use, and so it must be assumed to have performed *some* valuable function. Perhaps it was rather like "elections" in totalitarian countries, where a single list is present for approval to the "electorate", and duly voted into power, thus re-legitimizing the system. Perhaps this too was a simple ritual, in which clans and agnatic groups could ritually express their cohesion and solidarity?

Not so. In fact, strange though this may seem, the collective oath was no empty, predetermined form, there was genuine tension in the process (and the preliminary negotiations could result in a settlement "out of shrine", as you might say).

How then did it work? The official answer, as stated, is: fear of the supernatural. Strong as the call of loyalty to kin group is, there is a countervailing force – fear of the transcendent. Caught between loyalty to agnates and fear of supernatural sanction, the tribesman will, at least on occasion, be swayed by fear rather than loyalty. That is the "internal" theory, accepted by the participants, and all too often taken over uncritically by outside observers and interpreters .

I do not believe in this explanation, though it is part of the "internal" understanding of the system, and has indeed frequently been taken over by external observers and interpreters. Faith in the transcendent and fear thereof is a strange thing: it is often strong, and it would be wrong to credit populations with some kind of modern scepticism. Yet at the same time, it is not strong enough to determine conduct. How could populations who believed in hellfire, nonetheless sin, and sin so much? The pleasures of this world are considerable and I for one would not spurn them, but all things considered, if the price of enjoying them is eternal roasting, I for one would (regretfully) give up mundane joys. At least I think so: lacking the required faith in the coming of the sanctions in question, my *Gedankenexperiment* lacks authority. Hypothetical, imagined fears, dangers, or indeed temptations, have none of the force of *real* ones. All one can say is that real believers do not always behave as if their real beliefs inspired sufficiently real terror in their hearts. Bernard Shaw, in a play which he set in the very country and region in which we are at present meeting (*Captain Brassbound's Conversion*) makes one of his characters observe that the local tribesmen will not shoot any visiting infidel, even though they believe such an act will secure them entry to heaven, just as Christians do not generally give their wealth to the poor, even if they believe it will have the same effect.

Faith, like patriotism, is not enough. What then?

It is necessary to look at the logic of the situation of these nested, uncentralized, fairly egalitarian agnatic groups. It is important to remember that there is an absence of centralization, of enforcement agencies, not merely *between* these groups in conflict, but equally, *within* each one of them. There are conflicts and disagreements and tensions within each group, as well as between them. Westerners tend to think of tribes as mini-states. Some of them are, but this does not apply to the kind of tribal organization we are considering at present. Here there is very little by way of specialized coercive order-enforcing agency, at any level. The society "segments" into unspecialized sub-groups, and they in turn sub-divide in a similar manner. At each level of size, there are very *similar* groups, facing each other, encouraging each other to police their own members by fear of collective retaliation – but without special order-maintaining agents. There are "chiefs", but they are weak, not endowed with power or authority other than such as flows from moral support accorded by fellow members of the group.

Assume now that the accusation is made against a person who is a member of a highly cohesive group, and moreover, that he is a member in good standing, fully approved by his fellows, possessed of their confidence and support. In such a case, they will indeed stand by him and testify him out of his predicament. But it is precisely in such a case that it is least desirable to proceed to the next step, and begin a feud. This group is strong and cohesive, and so, hardly an attractive object of aggression. In such a case, when discretion is the better part of valour, the oath offers the accusing group a way out without loss of face. They accept the verdict of the oath, not, they say, because they are frightened of the group of the accused (perish the thought), but from simple piety: the shrine, or the deity, or some combination of the two, has assumed responsibility of the verdict, by not punishing those who testified in the process, and it is not for pious believers like us to stand out against the divine or the transcendent. The acceptance of the verdict is credited to piety, not weakness or fear.

But conviction and cohesion amongst the group of the accused is but one possibility. They may be internally divided, as often happens, and have grave doubts about the moral integrity of the accused. They may privately believe, not merely that he is guilty, but, more important, that his conduct is in character, and that his disposition to perform similar acts will lead them not merely to further oaths, but in all probability, to painful and frequently lethal feuds, with the groups of the aggrieved victims of their own kinsman. In an extreme case of such conviction, they may themselves take the offender into a wood and kill him. Within the moral-legal system of the tribesmen, there is indeed such a thing as laudable fratricide. The kin group itself should eliminate trouble-makers in its own midst. In a society without central authority, a group may do *unto itself* whatever it chooses, without committing an offence. By eliminating a trouble-maker in its own midst, it may be performing a morally laudable act. In the absence of specialized law-enforcing agencies, *only* the constituent sub-groups are available to enforce morality, whether against others or against themselves. The parallel with international order is obvious. Interference in "internal affairs" is generally held to be improper, and in any case impolitic.

But that is an extreme measure. They may not yet be willing to go as far as to break up the group or to kill one of its members. That would be the very last resort. In the meantime, there is an alternative, without quite such irreversible consequences. One can let the alleged culprit down at the oath, or at least, threaten to do so, by lukewarmness in the preparations for the oath and the negotiations which precede it.

121

The group can subsequently be restored, on a new basis, with the demonstration by one part of it that they will not indefinitely or unconditionally support certain kinds of conduct on the part of another member. But once again, failure to display full cohesion can be presented, not as weakness, but as piety. It is not so much that the supernatural enforces good conduct through fear: it makes both good conduct and rational calculation more possible, by providing them with a cover of piety.

It is something like this which, in my belief, really explains the nature of that widespread and fascinating institution, trial by collective oath. One can sum it all up as follows: the institution operates a kind of compromise between right and might. It is not an example of totally abstract justice, implementing a principle with indifference to the strength of the contestants. If a contestant is really strong, it recognizes that, in the absence of overarching superior force, it is quite useless to record a verdict against such a strong contestant. The verdict could not possibly be enforced, and the existence of such un-enforced justice would only bring justice itself into disrepute. This weakens the social order and respect for morality. So Might does receive a certain recognition. But not an exclusive one. It is normal, in political and military conflict, for the power situation to be less than wholly clear. It is not quite evident who will win, if it really comes to outright conflict. In the meantime, in a situation in which the balance of power is not fully visible, the merits of the case will at least have some influence on the behaviour of participants. If the case is really cogent, those supporting it will be more determined. If the case is weak, this may have some effect on the resolution of those identified with it. In situations which are less than clear from the viewpoint of force, Right too might then get a look in. So, in the end, the actual verdicts emerging from this procedure have a kind of variable sensitivity to both Might and Right: in a difficult and less than ideal world, this is perhaps as much as we can hope for.

Variants of the system described occur so frequently, that I for one am more inclined to explain it as a natural and common reaction to the logic of the situation than as a result of diffusion. It is more an emanation of a certain kind of organization, than a cultural trait which was accidentally invented in one place and then spread by contagion. That, at least, would be my guess. Something similar may operate even in centralized states, in zones of behaviour where the state, for one reason or another, is unwilling or reluctant to interfere: for instance, in industrial conflict. The logic of *strikes* is similar to that of collective oath: the outcome depends to a large extent on the degree of cohesion and conviction on the part of the contestants. These will only become evident when the strike actually takes place, but anticipation will influence the willingness to come to terms, and the nature of the terms

In support of this conjecture, I would invoke the very similar pattern which emerges in other loosely organized political systems, endowed with order but not endowed with an effective central law-enforcing agency. The international order as it has crystallized since the second World War is one such system. There is no supreme authority which could enforce any decision against the members of the United Nations: the UN only has such force as is composed of the forces of its member states, or groups of member states. The members are organized in groups or alliances or blocks, in effect, clans: membership is not strictly for keeps, but a change of alignment is a publicly noted fact. There are invariably tensions and conflicts within alliances/ clans as well as between them, and these internal stresses are crucial for the playing out of the larger conflicts.

One occasion on which one could observe something markedly similar to the tribal collective oath took place in 1956. At the time, certain members of the Western clan – to be precise, Britain, France, and Israel – were contemplating an act of aggression against another party, Egypt. So, apart from the wider conflict, there was also an internal tension within the Western block, some of whose members (including its leader, the USA) were not in sympathy with the act of aggression about to be committed by this internal sub-clan. However, the members of the sub-clan, fully aware of the disapproval of their plan felt by some (and consequently, keeping the plan secret and above all not admitting their prior collusion), nevertheless relied on the expectation that, when in the end it came to the collective oath at the UN shrine on Manhattan, the interests of clan loyalty would prevail over other interests, notably over mere moral indignation. In the event, this calculation proved to be incorrect. The other members of the super-clan decided to discipline their fellow members, who had overrated both their financial strength and their military effectiveness, and had to withdraw. The Western alliance did not come to an end. The chastened aggressors, who had been let down at the collective oath, had no option but to remain within the clan. (There had of course been internal divisions within some of them about the wisdom and/or the morality of the act which had provoked the crisis in the first place.) Or again, in the Gulf war, the lack of support for Saddam by many members of the Arab state clan, was decisive in making collective action possible. One clan was cohesive and another one was not, and the merit of the case had some influence on this.

The fact that, in loosely organized, uncentralized systems, constituents need to be organized in larger groups known as clans or blocks, and practise clan or block loyalty, does *not* mean that such loyalty, even if loudly proclaimed, will override all else. The simultaneous presence of conflicts at a whole number of levels, and the interactions of these various levels, ensures that on occasion participants will act not along clannish lines, but in accordance with other considerations. This arises from the logic of the situation, and not from some over-whelming force of piety or superstition or morality. A segmentary system works by occasional realignment, just as a market works by price changes.

As stated, international politics are not the only area in which one can find parallels to the collective oath, methods of conflict resolution which are all at once sensitive to the merits of the case and to the strength and resolution of the parties, without being exclusively sensitive to either one of these two types of concern. Strikes, obviously, often have a similar logic: much depends on the strength of the two parties in conflict, but much also on the genuineness of their conviction of the rightness of their case. The probing for weakness that takes place in the negotiations and manoeuvrings prior to outright confrontations are meant to test these.

The creation of an international sovereign, strong enough to implement decisions without regard to the cooperation of the units composing international society, is still something in the future – perhaps the very distant future. So, in the meantime, we can expect international decisions to be enforced by a mechanism which, even if its rituals and formal rationalizations are different, nevertheless in its inner logic strongly resembles tribal collective oath. Genuine conviction and a-moral loyalty to group both contribute to firmness of alignment and willingness to stand up and be counted. *Might or Right* is a false disjunction: loose social systems exist, amongst tribes as in an international community, which are responsive to *both*. This may not be ideal, but it is better than nothing.

Chapter 6

Keeping a Fractured Peace

Johan Jørgen Holst[1]

Seeking Common Ground

The issues discussed in this volume span a broad range of core questions in relation to the functioning of the international system, its structure, rules and inequities. Many of the issues remain open and do not lend themselves to resolution and settlement. Others have been more sharply delineated, defined and analysed. Not surprisingly the discussion unfolded in a tension field between description and prescription, between the world as we see it and the world as we would like it. The two poles sometimes converge as prescriptive perspectives and influence the organization of facts and projection of trends.

There is no disputing the proposition that the world is undergoing basic change, that we are in a period of transition, *in via*. However, the direction and pace of change are veiled in ambiguity. The future remains uncertain. Perceptions diverge and vary; realism mixes with idealism, wishful thinking with fatalistic thinking. Accurate description collides with equitable prescription.

The Structure of the Predicament

In assessing the premises for the commitment of military forces in the contemporary world we have to take as our point of departure the structure of international society. The security dilemma faced by states is rooted in that structure. No central authority exists for the international enforcement of standards and rules. Power remains decentralized and its distribution unequal. States remain the custodians of a fragile and frequently fractured peace. Nevertheless, certain "rules of the game" have been established and adhered to because their observance is in the interest of the principal states, and because they embody and project values which are central to the ethos of the time and to the social order contained by the states. Institutional norms and practices have been established for the purpose of mediating between might and right in order to establish and maintain minimum world order.[2]

It is not accepted then that might makes right. But right frequently is suppressed and violated by might. Standards and expectations change over time. The role and power of the state have become constrained and circumscribed by transnational trends and forces, including the spread of ethical norms, particularly in regard to human rights.

The Ethical Modification

If war is possible, the question arises if it is ever morally acceptable. The absolute pacifist says no. War inevitably implies destruction, the suffering and killing of human beings, a violation of the work of creation. The very nature of war makes it unacceptable. However, if war is evil, how do we combat evil? If war is imposed through aggression, do states have a right of self-defence? Yes, says the main body of international law, states possess an inherent right of self-defence. If they did not, the aggressive impulse would be unconstrained, evil would be rewarded and likely to encompass international society and dominate the human condition. Hence, the right of self-defence is necessary for order and justice to prevail.

127

It is not the act of war that is evil. War may be justified provided there be a just cause and a right intent. Self-defence is the only just cause, and a restoration of the *status quo ante* the only right intent according to international law.

St. Augustine thought differently. He accepted that turning the other cheek was the best way to break spirals of expanding violence, escalation in the modern vocabulary. However, he saw a moral obligation to assist the neighbour who had been subjected to aggression. Intervention on his behalf was justified and Thomas Aquinas considered it the duty of the righteous ruler. Wars were just if fought in defence, in order to retake something wrongly taken or in punishment of transgression. Roman law and international law revolve around the same themes.

Such rules are necessary for the maintenance of minimum world order, and in the absence of minimum world order evil would reign unencumbered. If aggression should not be resisted now, it is likely to be repeated and expanded tomorrow. We cannot only consider the evil aspects of the act of war, but we must also consider the consequences of not combating them. Hence, there is a *jus ad bellum*, a justice of war.

However, just cause and right intent are not sufficient conditions for the employment of military force to be legitimate and just. Wars have to be conducted within certain bounds. Violence should never be applied indiscriminately. There is also a *jus in bello*, a justice in war. The employment of force should be discriminate and proportional to the ends sought. Combat should be with combatants. Maximum violence is not permitted even if it could hasten the termination of war.[3] Hence, the juxtaposition of *jus ad bellum* and *jus in bello* project the classical tension between ends and means. The dilemma has become starker with the existence of nuclear weapons. It is the nature of the means and the expected consequences of their employment which results in a breakdown of the old categories. They have the capacity for indiscriminate destruction. But even more importantly, their effects extend beyond immediate destruction of contemporary human beings and their possessions. They threaten destruction of the genetic and ecological conditions of future human beings and their environment, the very work of creation.[4]

Nuclear Dilemmas

The system of nuclear deterrence emerged as a means to cope with the awesome capacity of nuclear weapons and the impossibility of their disinvention. That system contained and instituted new ethical dilemmas. It is hardly a good system or a durable solution. Instead, nuclear deterrence was a temporary expedient reflecting the imperfect arrangement of a world of seemingly sovereign and suspicious states. States threaten evil in order not to do it. Doing it would be so terrible that threatening it in order to prevent it seems to be morally defensible. However, if the threat is to deter, it has to be credible. The ultimate test of credibility is a will and ability to execute it. Fortunately a credible capacity for execution also implies a capacity to hold action. What would be morally unacceptable would be to so arrange nuclear forces that the response would be either automatic – in order to maximize deterrence – or carried out in anticipation in order to prevent disarming attacks.

The tenuous system of mutual nuclear deterrence is hardly a supreme monument to human ingenuity and compassion. Its simple but twisted logic must be transformed and transcended in order for the good in man to prevail, for him to build the good society. It seems to me that the only possible way is to change the nature of international society, reduce the role of the state and build transnational communities which are able to institute common security rather than competitive security. However, such transformation will take time and in the meantime the expedient must be maintained and modified in order to reduce the chance of accident and breakdown. However, since the knowledge about nuclear weapons cannot be erased, since they are relatively cheap, and since injustice and tension continue to shape the lives of a majority of the human race, the proliferation of nuclear weapons to new states remain a clear and present danger. Ultimate catastrophe remains latent in the human condition.

Nuclear weapons have shattered the relation between just

purpose and acceptable means, between *jus ad bellum* and *jus in bello*. Since modern war inevitably will be fought in the shadows of nuclear holocaust, under the potential for nuclear escalation, must we then conclude that even defensive war, armed resistance to aggression, has become morally unacceptable? I believe not, though clearly increased attention must be paid to *jus in bello*, to the means of war in order to minimize destruction and the danger of escalation.

In the absence of such means good states could become the victims of extortion from evil states. International relations could deteriorate to a macabre game of chicken. We have to develop alternatives to nuclear weapons, as well as alternative ways of employing military force to that of the forceful eviction of an aggressor. Force must be employed indirectly as well as discriminately within prescribed rules and against proscribed action. In order to defend values, we need justifiable means for defending them. Should we fail to do so, we might either be unable to defend basic values or be forced to do so in a manner which would in itself violate the values to be defended. Not all challenges to basic values need be apocalyptic. They are more likely than not to be limited and incremental. However, even peripheral and incremental violations could accumulate to systemic challenges if they are not constrained and punished in their incipiency. Appeasement seldom secures the peace. It is from the perspective of such dilemmas we have to view the practice of international peacekeeping, and its further evolution and refinement.

The Paradoxes of Power

In his approach to the use of force, moral man has to exercise extreme caution in the current condition of immoral society, to use the categories of Reinhold Niebuhr.[5] Relevant power has become more complex.

The translation of military capability into operationally relevant currency is becoming more complicated than in the past. In part this is due to the self-negating quality of nuclear weapons. In part it is a function of the inability of states to establish proportionality between the employment of weapons of mass destruction and political objectives in limited conflicts. The employment of incommensurate military force is constrained by the values of the societies which possess the weapons and by the threat of retaliation, not absolutely and reliably, but, till now, reasonably and tenuously. In the shadows of negated power, the weak may exploit the power of the strong to his benefit. Jiu-jitsu tactics may to some extent bridge the gap. The impotence of power is also part of the emerging reality. In addition, states confront the dilemmas created by the volatility of the societies which they contain, or often fail to contain. Struggle and violence, particularly in the third world, but also in what used to be the second world, follow indigenous routes, a logic beyond the regulatory influence of international deterrence and compellence. Power does not translate easily into authority or influence. Specific military capabilities do not invariably form instruments which can shape and constrain the behaviour of other actors in the international system. Power is becoming both dispersed and diffused and it does not grow out of the barrel of every gun around.

Emerging Instabilities

The Cold War order may not have been particularly pleasant and equitable, but it attained remarkable stability. The balance of nuclear deterrence turned out not to be as delicate as some predicted. Its very robustness created room for manoeuvre for the non-custodians of the balance. The lines were clearly drawn. Hence clarity rather than ambiguity, rigidity rather than fluidity, predictability rather than uncertainty constituted salient characteristics. With the demise of the Cold War and the attendant dissolution of the Warsaw Pact and the Soviet Union, the framework of international relations has changed fundamentally. The changes affect both leverage, incentives and propensities.

We should not, however, indulge in unwarranted nostalgia about the alluring clarity of the Cold War system. It is necessary to recall the awesome stakes and dangers it involved; the militarization of international relations, the debilitating impact of a military confrontation, the chilling shadows of nuclear conflagration, the enslavement of millions of people. With the end of the Cold War the war machines are being dismantled, the danger of nuclear war recedes, people regain a freedom lost or stolen. An ethos of cooperation is spreading, a new Europe is in the making, human freedom inspires goals for the future. Large scale war has ceased to constitute a clear and present danger.

The major powers no longer perceive local conflicts and rivalries from the perspective of a dominant struggle, as aspects or extensions of an ever expanding zero-sum game. Losses for one side do not translate into gains for the adversary when the adversarial relationship has been abandoned or transformed. The tail of client states cannot as before wag the bodies of their protectors. Leverage has been redistributed. The withering away of a global struggle could, of course, remove the constraints on the state or coalition which won the Cold War, tempt it or they into interventionist adventures unencumbered by the countervailing power of Moscow. On the other hand it could also cause the industrial nations to turn inward and away from engagement in the affairs and development of the third world, concentrate on internal or domestic priorities and on transforming the competitive relationship with the second world into cooperative endeavours. Collusion and connivance could be the result, but also aloofness and disengagement.

The stalemate of the Cold War provided a framework and basis for minimum order. The threat of intervention and engagement restrained the behaviour of third parties. In the post-Cold War era an ethos of order through coercion or its virtual equivalents may be replaced by an ethos of commerce or *laissez-faire*. The impact on the maintenance and management of minimum world order remains ambiguous and uncertain, particularly since we may see a growing cleavage between the prevailing ethos of the prosperous north and that of the impoverished south. We may also see cleavages and divisions within the north with regard to the prevailing ethos.

The withering away of the global struggle could act as an incentive for proliferation of weapons of mass destruction and the means for their rapid delivery over long distances. Local struggles and ambitions may be rekindled, deepened and expanded in the post-Cold War era. The cohesion of the clan which won the Cold War may diminish, but even more dramatic would be the break up or demise of the non-aligned movement. It has largely lost its *raison d'être* and point of reference with the disappearance of the two competing alliances. We are likely to see a break up of the tenuous unity of the third world, its differentiated accommodation and linkage to the victorious first world clan. The latter remains dependent on some of the resources of the former, most notably oil, but the third world countries' dependence on access to the economic system of the first world affects the distribution of leverage and incentives for exploiting market positions. Oil constitutes a case *sui generis* and is likely to forge strong links and patterns of engagement between the countries of the Middle East and the first-world countries. The calls for a new economic order may become muted as regions or groupings of countries of the third world form clans which seek relations with and even cooption into the economic system of the first world.

A reordering of the international economic system would have to be motivated by a sense of equity which till now has not permeated actual policy, but been confined to the declaratory level of politics. Or it could be inspired by an enlightened sense of long term interests. But that seems no less remote than the former possibility. The environmental condition linking the north and the south to a common future could inspire states of the first and third world to view their policy choices and interests from the perspective of a single system of growing interdependence. However, cultural differences between the two worlds, particularly in regard to the core values of the first world, and especially those relating to human rights, could generate tension and reinforce propensities for intervention in the third world. Integration is likely to broaden awareness, deepen responsibility and legitimate engagement.

The Elusive Concept of Sovereignty

The role of intervention and peacekeeping in international relations naturally proceeds from an assessment of the state of international society. It remains unclear whether we are heading for increased international anarchy or a more integrated international community. Both trends are discernable at present.

Any assessment of the structure and processes of the international system and the ethical premises for participating in international conflicts has to include and embrace the concept of sovereignty; the properties, imperatives and mutations involved. Are we witnessing the subduing of sovereignty or its restoration? Will the jealous protection of exclusive authority continue to characterize the major if not the only "game in town"?

What are indeed the properties or attributes of sovereignty? Do they extend beyond the effective and the near exclusive control of a defined territory, or do they include also requirements for legitimate government, reflecting some kind of contract between rulers and the ruled, a concept of legitimate government? Who has the right to claim and contest sovereignty?

In European political history the concept of sovereignty constituted a political response to ecclesiastical authority in the early 15th century. It was not dependent on any national identity or popular will. Legitimacy was decided by dynastic rulers and derived from feudal law, the monarch and the sovereign coincided. In the words of Jean Bodin, "The attributes of sovereignty are therefore peculiar to the sovereign prince, for if communicable to the subject, they cannot be called attributes of sovereignty."[6] Following the American and French Revolutions the legal and historical state had to yield to the nation state and the concept of the sovereignty of "the people".

Since then Western political thought has linked the concept of sovereignty to notions of legitimate government, to the contractual conditions for the right to rule. However, international law has tended to focus on the reality of rule rather than the quality of rule. If the right to self determination and statehood applies to political communities, it may be doubted that the claim to sovereignty can be upheld when a government turns savagely upon its own people. Such a government has only tenuous claims to be accepted as a legitimate expression of a political community. In such instances humanitarian interventions may be justified in terms of constituting a response to an evil which cannot be tolerated by the moral conscience of mankind. We postulate here an authority beyond the realm of the state, and that postulate remains controversial in contemporary international relations. Increasingly, however, in the words of Michael Walzer, "we praise or don't condemn these violations of the formal rules of sovereignty, because they uphold the values of individual life and communal liberty of which sovereignty itself is merely an expression".[7]

The authority of the state is subject to the many obligations of international law expressed through treaties, customary law, juridical postulates and accepted standards of the international community. Nevertheless, international society remains divided also in relation to the understanding of sovereignty, particularly with regard to legitimacy, or the constitution and practice of legitimate government. It has sometimes been suggested that the post-Cold War order may be described in terms of a Kantian core embracing most of the first world and a Hobbesian periphery encompassing mainly the third world. The two spheres interact and we are bound to see defection and cross-overs in both directions. However, the ethos and values of the agricultural societies of the south may continue to diverge systematically and saliently from those of the commercial and industrial societies of the north, the former being more disposed to accept effective government by coercion.

It is possible also to view the dilemma from another direction: How do we mediate the relation between the traditional notion of the inviolability of the borders of the territorial state on the one hand and the emerging notion of the inviolability of the individual on the other? Do human beings acquire human rights by the mere fact of belonging to the human race or are the rights of man only to be conceived of as the rights of citizens? How do we choose between Thomas Paine and Jean Jacques Rousseau? What are the implications of the choice on the behaviour of states and the rules of their game? No consensus prevails. International law is in evolution and the fact and activities of non-state actors transform and mediate its traditional focus on the rights and duties of states. But what are their rights and duties beyond borders? Could professions of ideological commitment to defend the rights of man, to protect attempts at humanitarian assistance, be viewed by the majority of states as camouflaged intervention into their internal affairs? How do we prevent intervention and peace-keeping from turning into conquest?

Sovereignty may in fact be waning more rapidly than widely presumed, assuming the mantle of a myth rather than demonstrable properties. One basic aspect of the concept of sovereignty was the presumption of exclusive authority. Today no state can claim or enjoy such authority. States can only possess it by degrees, but if that be the case it no longer exists in its proclaimed form, for the concept applied to an absolute idea. The notion of limited sovereignty is in some sense a contradiction in terms. Nevertheless, that contradiction has become reality. Economic interdependence, the penetration of borders by technology, news and lifestyles constrain and delimit the exercise of sovereignty, of exclusive authority. People are increasingly being linked into broader communities, in contra-vention of the established notion of the sovereign territorial state as the constituent unit of international society.

The concept of sovereignty was tied logically to the ability to protect citizens and physical values against destruction by other sovereigns. The ability to protect has been eroded and diminished as a result of the development of military technology. Nuclear weapons, long range bombers and missiles have blown the roof off the territorial state. States are now linked together by a condition of mutual vulnerability rather than effective exclusion. The fiction of a protective shield was maintained during the Cold War era by the system of mutual nuclear deterrence. That system is now in the process of being dismantled and transformed. The condition of vulner-ability emerges with increased salience.[8]

Emerging Communities?

In Europe sovereignty is being tamed and transformed by a process of trans-national community building, linking local communities in broader associations, breaking the monopoly of the territorial state, making the latter less all-encompassing or less sovereign, creating multiple identities also across borders, transforming relations between citizens and societies, societies and states. Keeping the peace in Europe depends to a considerable degree on the creation of non-territorial cultural sovereignties within the context of an European community. Regional interests in stability and prosperity could conceivably contain and transform particularist interests.

However, beyond Europe the picture is less promising. The dialectic of rebellion and repression is likely to shape the future of many developing countries. In the wake of the dissolution of the Warsaw Pact and the Soviet Union, it is knocking at the gates of Europe as well. Peacekeeping in Europe has changed with the dismantlement of the confrontation which used to divide it. Some years ago we worried about the Balkanization of Lebanon. Today we are witnessing the Lebanonization of the Balkans. The disintegrating powers of nationalism and communal strife are not confined to the third world.

Most of the states in Europe are multinational states rather than nation states in an ethnic sense. But imagined communities may be forged around other myths than that of ethnicity. Nevertheless, the nineteenth century nationalist prescription that state borders should coincide with ethnic borders is manifestly impossible within the mosaic of human intermingling created through the millennia. In any event, it amounts to a prescription for perpetual war rather than perpetual peace. How do you bound the right to self-determination, prevent a process of constant fission into ever smaller sovereignties and conflicts among them? By what criteria is it possible to decide where imagined communities should be allowed to form states, claim territoriality?

With the end of the Cold War the United Nations is able to function as envisaged in San Francisco in 1945. However, the world of the 1990s is not like the world of 1945. A world run by the leaders of the war-time coalition from the Second World War will be resented and resisted by a majority of the states which now make up the United Nations in the post-colonial era. The future of international peacekeeping depends on the ability to alter the rules and practices with regard to decision-making in order to make them more consistent with the presumption of the equality of states. We know that to be a fiction, of course, albeit a useful fiction, an ideal standard by which to judge the inequities of an imperfect system. To some extent the United Nations' rules and practices reflect a real distribution of power and it could be seriously weakened and marginalized were it not to be reflected in an approximate way.

It is sometimes suggested that the world is becoming increasingly unified by universal values. However, distinctions must be made between values which are universally accepted and values which claim universal validity. Unfortunately it seems rather doubtful that the states in the international system are becoming increasingly committed to a single set of values, even if a certain amount of lip service is paid to those values when they are considered from the perspective of general principles rather than operational imperatives.

From Intervention to Peacekeeping

The subduing of sovereignty may imply a lowering of the threshold for intervention by promoting integration and community building. Intervention remains a rather diffuse concept. It is always a matter of degree. It may take place by a variety of means for the projection of outside influence into the space of a territorial state. The means may range from statements, broadcasts and newspapers at the low end of the spectrum through foreign aid – particularly when tied to conditionality – to economic measures – even sanctions, to protection of humanitarian assistance, to demonstration or use of armed force, to full-fledged invasion at the high end. They pierce the protective shields of the territorial state, modify the exclusive authority of its government and affect attitudes and behaviour. Intervention by armed forces has been the traditional source of concern and condemnation. The future incidence of such intervention is wrapped in ambiguity due, in part, to the uncertainties about north-south relations. However, armed intervention is not confined to intervention of the first into the third world. It could take place inside the third world by third world powers as well as inside the first world by first world powers. Legitimacy will always be a contested issue with regard to armed intervention. The issue is not resolved by requiring the request or consent by the government into whose sovereign space intervention is made, as the legitimacy of government itself may be far from clear and manipulated from the outside. Puppet governments hardly qualify as repositories of sovereignty.

Moreover, increasingly governmental power will fission or dissipate, become contested and eroded as states are torn asunder by the fervour of ethnic conflict. Intervention may be attempted in order to prevent anarchy from consuming societies to the point of eradicating any framework of authority and regulated community. The conflict in Bosnia-Herzegovina in the last decade of the twentieth century is an awesome reminder that the ideological forces that almost destroyed Europe twice during the last 100 years have retained their popular appeal and mobilizing power. The pursuit of ethnic cleansing implies a dehumanization of "other" citizens, a reduction to the absurd of the notion of the exclusive community. The quest for sovereignty based on ethnic purity is, to a large extent, incompatible with maintaining a minimum world order based on tolerance and mutual respect.

States intervene into the affairs of other states to protect and pursue their national interests in order to obtain influence and control or deny these to competing states. They may also intervene in order to prevent a collapse of regional stability and to reinforce the rules, norms and standards upon which that stability is grounded. The Conference on Security and Cooperation in Europe, the CSCE, embodies and projects such rules and standards. The conflict in Bosnia-Herzegovina constitutes a direct challenge to that very construction. Nevertheless, states have been manifestly unwilling to intervene. The reasons are manifold. Vital interests do not seem to be engaged. Success is difficult to define and attain. Moreover, states are immobilized by, appropriate or inappropriate, historical memories and analogies (the "Vietnam quagmire"). Finally, there is a lack of willingness to sustain casualties in conflicts that have little direct bearing on critical national interests. Although most people might be ready to demonstrate in defense of civilized principles of behaviour, very few seem disposed to die for them.

Accusations of double standards resound as critics point to the difference between reactions to the crises in Somalia, the Sudan and Bosnia. However, states have never adhered to the imperative of a single standard. It borders on sophistry to argue that states cannot intervene anywhere because they will not intervene everywhere. States have always been selective in their reactions to international crises, even if the human suffering involved would seem to require action as a matter of morality.

States may intervene then for a variety of reasons beyond greed and the pursuit of unilateral advantage. They may want to stop a process of falling dominoes (the crisis management perspective), prevent undesirable precedents (the preventive perspective), safeguard human rights (the humanitarian perspective), protect essential norms and standards (the minimum order perspective) or maintain authority (the systemic perspective).

The search for legitimate intervention includes the concept of international peacekeeping, a functional substitute for unilateral and self-styled armed intervention. It projects the idea of collective action as envisaged by the Charter of the United Nations, not necessarily and invariably as a multilateral undertaking, but as an undertaking which is authorized by the United Nations under agreed command and control, and operating according to collectively agreed procedures and rules of engagement.

After the end of the Cold War the states of Europe and North America are moving away from permanent military readiness and forward deployment to an emphasis on reconstitution and rapid reaction. The Western coalition which emerged victorious from the Cold War now emphasizes multinational formations in order to prevent a renationalization of defences. This reorientation of military forces is designed in part to enhance the capacity for international peacekeeping. Peacekeeping has entered a new era. The process involves some important transformations. In order to encompass their scope and implications, we have to move from general considerations to particular prescriptions.

A New Era of Peacekeeping

Second or third generation peacekeeping is more variegated and complex in its manifestations and requirements than those of the first generation, the UNEF-generation, as we could call it. They are still in a process of gestation. They could transcend the requirements for consent by the parties affected.

Modern peacekeeping may range from fact-finding missions through observer missions, verification of arms control agreements, ballot supervision, interposition, truce supervision, force separation, to protection of humanitarian assistance. Peacekeeping in this sense requires and is predicated on the consent of the parties involved, on their preference for peace but need for an outside agent to monitor and verify compliance with arrangements for cease-fire or disengagement. Peacekeeping in this sense constitutes action undertaken under Chapter VI of the Charter of the United Nations, "Pacific Settlement of Disputes".

Three major problems arise in connection with peacekeeping: 1) Peacekeeping tends to become a means for taking issues off the diplomatic agenda, for putting conflicts into the deep freeze rather than moving them towards solution. 2) In many modern conflicts it is difficult to identify the parties involved. They tend to fission and multiply, to change the cast of characters and their interplay during the course of peacekeeping operations. Hence, the consent of the parties involved often becomes a moving target making it difficult for the peacekeepers not to be viewed as another party to the conflict by at least some of the parties actually involved. 3) In order to be viewed as credible, disinterested parties peacekeepers have come primarily from smaller and medium powers. However, the emphasis on neutrality in many instances reduce their ability to deter challenges to the peace they seek to maintain. Participation of the great powers could have enhanced deterrence as well as the authority of the mandating institution. Keeping the great powers out of peacekeeping was necessary in order to prevent local conflicts from becoming extensions of the Cold War. Now that concern has vanished.

Peacekeeping operations should be distinguished then from peacemaking operations, or enforcement action under Chapter VII of the UN Charter, "Action with Respect to Threats to the Peace, Breaches of Peace, and Acts of Aggression". Peacemaking operations may range from preventive deployments, through police action, enforced disarmament of particular weapons and forces, protection of key installations and authorities, to collective intervention. Although there is a grey zone between peacekeeping and peacemaking the two remain distinctly different. Peacemaking was generally prevented by the absence of great power consensus upon which action under Chapter VII was predicated. The Korean War was an exception and "Desert Storm" became possible for reasons which are hardly generally duplicable, even after the end of the Cold War.

It is possible for specific regions to constitute special regional arrangements under Chapter VIII of the UN Charter, also for dealing with matters relating to the maintenance of international peace and security, including appropriate regional action. This is the development many countries now envisage and seek with regard to the CSCE. If the CSCE is to develop into a security community, it must be able to undertake peacekeeping operations as well. However, like children, international institutions must learn to walk before they attempt to run. Peacekeeping should precede peacemaking.

Peacekeeping provides mechanisms and frameworks for transforming national or multinational military formations into instruments of collective action. Many states of the industrialized north focus on the creation of expeditionary forces with high mobility and fire power now that the requirement to man a front line of confrontation has been removed. Such capacities constitute insurance against unspecified dangers in an uncertain world. They could provide, of course, the means for offensive intervention as well as for defensive protection. They could provide building-blocks or components of multinational peacekeeping operations under the auspices of the United Nations, regional organizations or both. Such tasks would tend to change the role of armed forces as protectors of sovereignties which have long since ceased to be sovereign and instead become instruments for the maintenance of minimum world order in accordance with collectively agreed norms and standards.

The two functions are not necessarily incompatible and the assignment of national formations to collective peacekeeping operations could reduce the security dilemmas created by the acquisition and operation of military forces by territorial states in a semi-anarchical international system. The parallel existence and prosecution of legitimate and illegitimate armed intervention undoubtedly will continue to generate tension and controversy. However, the mere existence and practice of a legitimate alternative could temper propensities and incentives to resort to intervention, particularly in open societies. Internationalizing the role of military forces, in addition, could have an important socializing effect on the armed forces of the former Soviet Union, particularly since they have been the traditional custodians of a concept of hostility, xenophobia, vis-a-vis the outside world, of fear of encirclement and invasion, of estrangement and separation.

Making PeaceKeeping Work

For peacekeeping to become institutionalized it has to develop its particular identity and attributes, its uniqueness in relation to other military operations. In addition it has to develop a certain institutional memory, paying attention to both continuity and change. Education and training constitute key activities in that connection. In order to translate general concepts into concrete action, we need to answer the Leninist question, *chto delat'*, or what's to be done? In order to encourage the search for answers, it could be useful to outline a possible scheme for developing an educational infrastructure for international peacekeeping, incremental in nature, but with the potential for promoting systemic change. A staged process could include the following elements:[9]

1. The establishment of an *international peacekeeping academy* for the evaluation and development of the techniques of peacekeeping, resulting in a set of tactical manuals, seminars on doctrine, workshops on the practice of peacekeeping, etc. It should be run by the United Nations, have a small permanent staff, resident fellows (mostly military officers with UN peacekeeping experience), visiting lecturers, etc.

2. Over time it could establish within its structure a *peacekeeping staff college* for senior military officers making it possible in due course to make such additional education a prerequisite for appointment to senior command positions in UN peacekeeping operations.

3. Furthermore, it is possible to envisage the establishment of a certain number of *UN regional training centres for peacekeeping* for junior and non-commissioned officers as well as private soldiers.

    The purpose of such a structure would be six-fold:

(a) To develop and formalize a set of relevant techniques of peacekeeping.

(b) Enhance the effectiveness of peacekeeping operations by increasing the chance that national contingents committed to such operations abide by a common set of standard operating procedures.

(c) Prevent the techniques of peacekeeping from atrophying into an inappropriate, dysfunctional conventional wisdom, the remnants of a past world. The Scandinavian-Canadian views on peacekeeping developed during the Cold War, the UNEF viewpoint, could, if they are not transcended and transformed, constrain peacekeepers from meeting their new tasks, making them victims of what Thorstein Veblen called trained incapacities.

(d) Provide a means for socializing military institutions, the traditional guardians of the territorial states and custodians of claims to sovereignty; institutions which are nation-builders, but also often potential coup-makers. Training in peacekeeping could inject into national militaries an international cooperative ethos in contrast to one of national competition. To a small, but not insignificant extent they could become instruments for transnational community building.

(e) Develop concepts of international military operations which are consistent with and promotive of the restraints on the use of force projected by the just war doctrine; the proportional response and discriminate application which reduce harm to innocent by-standers.

(f) Contribute to the execution of collective action, provide instruments and options for nations committed to the principles, prescriptions and proscriptions of the UN Charter.

Further institutionalization of peacekeeping may involve the establishment of regional UN logistical depots and a UN peacekeeping transportation organization comprising transport aircraft and logistic supply ships, initially perhaps through the assignment of such capabilities by nations to the UN on a stand-by, on-call basis.

The Road Ahead

We have entered a new era. Yet history threatens to return with vengeance, with a replay of nationalist struggles, communal strife and ethnic animosities. But we also have a chance to put history on a new course of collective action for common goals and expanded communities.

The old order based on sovereign states was constituted in Europe at the Peace of Westphalia in 1648 after the Thirty Years War. It became global following another thirty years of European wars from 1914–1945 as a result of which the European colonial empires were busted. Following more than forty years of Cold War a new order is in the making. Concepts of divisible and transferable sovereignty are propounded and implemented in Europe. Power is becoming more multidimensional and divisible, structures more complex and elastic and the territorial states more vulnerable and subject to outside manipulation.

Notes

1. Johan Jørgan Holst is the Minister of Foreign Affairs of Norway. The views expressed in this article are purely personal and do not necessarily reflect those of the Norwegian government.

2. For elaboration see Hedley Bull, *The Anarchical Society*. A Study of Order in World Politics, London, The Macmillan Press, Ltd, 1977 and Myres S McDougal and Florentino P Feliciano, *Law and Minimum World Public Order*, New Haven, Yale University Press, 1961.

3. See Geoffrey Best, *Humanity in Warfare*, New York, Columbia University Press, 1980 and Paul Ramsey, *The Just War*. Force and Political Responsibility, New York, Charles Scribner's Sons, 1968; James Turner Johnson, *Just War Tradition and the Restraint of War*. A Moral and Historical Inquiry, Princeton, N.J., Princeton University Press, 1981 and James Turner Johnson, *Can Modern War Be Just?*, New Haven, Yale University Press, 1984.

4. For further discussion see David Fisher, *Morality and the Bomb*. An Ethical Assessment of Nuclear Deterrence, London, Croom Helm, 1985; Gregory S Kavka, *Moral Paradoxes of Nuclear Deterrence*, Cambridge, Cambridge University Press, 1987; Joseph S Nye, Jr, *Nuclear Ethics*, New York, The Free Press, 1986.

5. Reinhold Niebuhr, *Moral Man and Immoral Society*, New York, Charles Scribner's Sons, 1932.

6. Quoted from Jean Bodin, *Six Books of the Commonwealth*, Oxford, Basil Blackwell, n.d. Book I, Chapter 10, p. 42.

7. Michael Walzer, *Just and Unjust Wars*. A Moral Argument with Historical Illustrations, Hammondsworth, Penguin Books, 1980, p. 108.

8. For a brilliant analysis see John H Herz, *International Politics in the Atomic Age*, New York, Columbia University Press, 1959, Particularly Part I.

9. See also Johan Jørgen Holst, "Enhancing Peacekeeping Operations", *Survival*, 32(3) May–June, 1990: 264–277.

INDEX

147

Subduing Sovereignty

W

Walzer, Michael, 84, 135
Warsaw Pact, 131, 137
Weber, Max, 69
Weinberger, Caspar, 74
· West Bank, 21, 27, 73, 74
Westphalia, Peace of, 145
Western Sahara, 27
World Bank, 63, 69, 85, 86,
    87, 88, 89
World War I, 19, 22, 23, 70
World War II, 17, 24, 36, 67,
    72, 123, 138

Y

Yugoslavia, 31, 53
    civil war in, 19, 29, 107
    former, 15, 51, 97, 98
    see also United Nations,
        intervention in